King Lear

by William Shakespeare

Martin Old

Series Editors:
Nicola Onyett and Luke McBratney

EDUCATION
AN HACHETTE UK COMPANY

The publisher would like to thank the following for permission to reproduce copyright material:

Acknowledgments:

pp.6, 13, 14, 16, 19, 21, 34, 41: Leo Tolstoy: from *Tolstoy on Shakespeare: A Critical Essay on Shakespeare* (Funk & Wagnalls, 1906); **p.24: G.K. Hunter:** from *King Lear* (Penguin, 2005); **p.27:** from 'What Is a Psychopath?' (Copyright © 1994–2009 Arkadiusz Jadczyk and Laura Knight-Jadczyk); www.cassiopaea.com; **p.27: Robert D. Hare:** from *Without Conscience: The Disturbing World of the Psychopaths Among Us* (Guildford Press, 1999); **p.48: Kirsty Lang:** from ''I get upset when I don't hear people gasping during the killings': King Lear's stellar cast gets ready to face the biggest audience of their careers' from *The Daily Mail* (The Daily Mail, 26th April 2014); **p.48: Charles Spencer:** from 'King Lear, National Theatre, review' from *The Telegraph* (The Telegraph, 23rd January 2014); **p.49: Leo Kirschbaum:** from *Character and Characterization in Shakespeare* (Holt, Rinehart and Winston, 1962); **p.49: Kenneth Muir:** from *Shakespeare's ''King Lear'' (Masterstudies)* (Penguin, 1986); **p.50: Jan Kott:** from *Shakespeare Our Contemporary* (Routledge, 1990); **p.58:** from the Yale University prospectus (Yale University, 2014); **p.65: William Shakespeare:** from *The History of King Lear: The Oxford Shakespeare*, ed. Stanley Wells (OUP, 2008); **p.67: Caroline Spurgeon:** from *Shakespeare's Imagery and What it Tells Us* (Martino Fine Books, 1935); **p.72: Ernst Cassirer:** from *The Individual and the Cosmos in Renaissance Philosophy* (University of Chicago Press, 1927); **p.74: Frank Kermode:** from *The Classic* (Viking Adult, 1975); **p.82: G.L. Evans:** from 'Shakespeare's Fools: The Shadow and Substance of Drama' from *Shakespearean Comedy*, eds. Malcolm Bradbury and David Palmer (Holmes & Meier, 1972); **p.82: Peter Thomson:** from *Shakespeare's Professional Career* (Cambridge University Press, 2010); **p.84: Frank Kermode:** from *Shakespeare: King Lear* (Palgrave Macmillan, 1992).

Every effort has been made to trace or contact all copyright holders, but if any have been inadvertently overlooked the Publishers will be pleased to make the necessary arrangements at the first opportunity.

Photo credits:

p.1 (left) © VisitBritain/LeeBeel/Getty images; **(right)** © GL Archive/Alamy; **p.14** © The British Library Board, Royal 2 A. XVI, f.63v; **p.19** © Wellcome Library, London / http://creativecommons.org/licenses/by/4.0/; **p.21** © Vyacheslav Volkov/123RF; **p.28** © Mark Douet; **p.29** © Ms 3045 fol.22v Boethius with the Wheel of Fortune, from 'De Consolatione Philosophiae', translated by Jean de Meung (vellum), French School, (15th century) / Bibliotheque Municipale, Rouen, France / Bridgeman Images; **p.46** © Hagg/Ullstein Bild/Getty Images; **p.48** © Mark Douet; **p.65** © The Horace Howard Furness Shakespeare Collection, Kislak Center for Special Collections, Rare Books and Manuscripts, University of Pennsylvania Libraries; **p.70** © Theodor de Bry/ Bettmann/Corbis; **p.71** © Cordelia Molloy/Science Photo Library

Although every effort has been made to ensure that website addresses are correct at time of going to press, Hodder Education cannot be held responsible for the content of any website mentioned. It is sometimes possible to find a relocated web page by typing in the address of the home page for a website in the URL window of your browser.

Orders: please contact Bookpoint Ltd, 130 Milton Park, Abingdon, Oxon OX14 4SB. Telephone: (44) 01235 827720. Fax: (44) 01235 400454. Lines are open 9.00–17.00, Monday to Saturday, with a 24-hour message answering service. Visit our website at www.hoddereducation.co.uk

© Martin Old, 2011, 2016

First published in 2016 by

Hodder Education

An Hachette UK Company,

Carmelite House, 50 Victoria Embankment

London EC4Y 0DZ

Impression number	5	4	3	2	1
Year	2020	2019	2018	2017	2016

Cover photo (and throughout) © nejron/123RF.com

Typeset in Univers LT Std 47 Light Condensed 11/13 pt by Integra Software Services Pvt. Ltd., Pondicherry, India

Printed in Italy

A catalogue record for this title is available from the British Library.

ISBN 9781471853869

Contents

Using this guide iv

Introduction 1

1 Synopsis 3

2 Scene summaries and commentaries 6

3 Themes 42

4 Characters 46

5 Writer's methods: Form, structure and language 53

6 Contexts 57

7 Working with the text 77

Assessment Objectives and skills 77

Building skills 1: Structuring your writing 79

Building skills 2: Analysing texts in detail 91

Extended commentary 97

Top ten quotations 100

Taking it further 105

The text used for this guide to *King Lear* is the 1997 Arden Shakespeare edited by R.A. Foakes; line references used in this guide refer to this edition.

Why read this guide?

The purposes of this A-level Literature Guide are to enable you to organise your thoughts and responses to the text, to deepen your understanding of key features and aspects, and to help you address the particular requirements of examination questions and non-examination assessment (NEA) tasks in order to obtain the best possible grade. It will also prove useful to those of you writing an NEA piece on the text as it provides a number of summaries, lists, analyses and references to help with the content and construction of the assignment.

Note that above all else teachers and examiners are seeking evidence of an *informed personal response to the text*. A guide such as this can help you to understand the text, form your own opinions, and suggest areas to think about, but it cannot replace your own ideas and responses as an informed and autonomous reader.

How to make the most of this guide

You may find it useful to read sections of this guide when you need them, rather than reading it from start to finish. For example, you may find it helpful to read the 'Contexts' section before you start reading the text, or to read the 'Scene summaries and commentaries' section in conjunction with the text – whether to back up your first reading of it at school or college or to help you revise. The sections relating to the Assessment Objectives will be especially useful in the weeks leading up to the exam.

This guide is designed to help you raise your achievement in your examination response to *King Lear*. It is intended for you to use throughout your AS/A-level English Literature course. It will help you when you are studying the play for the first time and also during your revision.

The following features have been used throughout this guide to help you focus your understanding of the play:

Context

Context boxes give contextual information that relates directly to particular aspects of the text.

Build critical skills

Broaden your thinking about the text by answering the questions in the **Build critical skills** boxes. These help you to consider your own opinions in order to develop your skills of criticism and analysis.

TASK

Tasks are short and focused. They allow you to engage directly with a particular aspect of the text.

Taking it further ▶▶

Taking it further boxes suggest and provide further background or illuminating parallels to the text.

CRITICAL VIEW

Critical view boxes highlight a particular critical viewpoint that is relevant to an aspect of the main text. This allows you to develop the higher skills needed to come up with your own interpretation of a text.

Top ten quotation

Top ten quotation

A cross-reference to a Top ten quotation (see pages 100–104 of this guide), where each quotation is accompanied by a commentary that shows why it is important.

There are at least two William Shakespeares that exist in the collective mind of the British public: there is the safe 'hey nonny nonny' Shakespeare, creator of charming rural plays and light but delicious love affairs, and inhabitant of thatched cottages in Warwickshire. This first Shakespeare is a conformist.

Then there is the second Shakespeare: experimental theatrical genius, rebellious intellectual and enigmatic habitué of London tap rooms and playhouses. These two views can be seen by the differing representations shown below. The one on the right known as the 'Chandos portrait', after a previous owner, was the first portrait to be acquired by the National Portrait Gallery when it was founded in 1856 and is perhaps the best known visual representation.

▲ Shakespeare's funerary monument from Holy Trinity Church, Stratford: more pork-butcher than playwright?

▲ This portrait of Shakespeare is the only one to have a good claim to have been painted from life, and may be by John Taylor of the Painter-Stainers' Company

King Lear is often cited as one of the greatest works of literature ever written: George Bernard Shaw wrote 'No man will ever write a better tragedy than *Lear*', but others have despised it in its entirety or have found elements of it deeply troubling. William Makepeace Thackeray, the Victorian novelist, wrote of a production he saw in 1847: 'It is almost blasphemy to say that a play of Shakespeare is bad; but I can't help it, if I think it is.' Even admirers of the playwright have found *King Lear* an alarming play. Henrik Schuck (1855–1947), a hugely influential Swedish critic, thought the play 'unworthy of Shakespeare, full of gory murder, bestial lust and madness and in regard to structure and motivation one of his weakest plays.' And thereby hangs a tale. *King Lear* presents such a dark view of life and human behaviour that it is profoundly shocking: the murders, maimings and mutilations are gory, the lust is bestial and the madness is unsettling. Some of the cruelties the playwright presents may appear to lack reason or motive. The play is certainly stark and terrifying. That does not, however, make *King Lear* bad. It is an unusual and remarkable play.

There is some evidence to suggest that Shakespeare revised *King Lear* at least once. Anthony Nuttall of Oxford University and Harold Bloom of Yale University have endorsed the view that Shakespeare revisited the play to change the theatrical experience. If we accept this view then we must also accept the fact that Shakespeare believed the play to be important to him both as a man and as a writer. There are some striking parallels between *King Lear*, *Othello*, *Timon of Athens* and *Measure for Measure*, which all date from roughly the same period in Shakespeare's career as a dramatist. The words 'besort', 'unbonnetted', 'waterish', 'deficient' and 'potential' are used by Shakespeare only in *Othello* and *King Lear*. The idea of an absent authority figure in the forms of the Duke and the King is common to *Measure for Measure* and *King Lear*. There is also a running debate on notions of justice, authority and punishment in *Measure for Measure* and *King Lear*, which both also make use of the phrase 'furred gown'. Parallel themes in *Timon of Athens* and *King Lear* include ingratitude, human life as comparable to the life of animals, and the inherent and natural goodness of the poor in contrast to the poisonous cruelty of the rich. Ideas about sexual impropriety and imagery of diseases and the human body also feature prominently in the plays of 1603–06, which some critics refer to as Shakespeare's 'Dark Phase'. Yet darkness can convey its own intense shadowy beauty.

The play is certainly one of Shakespeare's most intense, a fact picked up by poet John Keats (1795–1821), who seemed to understand the complexities of studying *King Lear* as well as anyone: 'The excellence of every art is in its intensity, capable of making all disagreeables evaporate, from their being in close relationship with Beauty and Truth. Examine *King Lear*, and you will find this exemplified throughout.'

The Earls of Gloucester and Kent enter, accompanied by Gloucester's illegitimate son Edmund. Gloucester informs Kent that the 'whoreson' Edmund must be 'acknowledged' as his. Then 80-year-old King Lear divides Britain into three parts, each to be governed by one of his daughters: Goneril and Regan, who are married to the Dukes of Albany and Cornwall respectively, and Cordelia, who is being courted by both the Duke of Burgundy and the King of France. Lear, worn out, feels that the responsibilities of ruling should be passed on to younger shoulders but arranges to retain one hundred knights as companions. Before he divides his kingdom, however, Lear asks each of his daughters how much she loves him. As Goneril and Regan try to outdo each other in exaggerated terms, Cordelia grows anxious: her nature is not given to making speeches about her deepest feelings. When her turn comes, Cordelia tells Lear that she loves him as a daughter 'according to my bond', but when she marries she will, of course, love her husband too. Her honest reply angers Lear, who disowns her, and splits his kingdom into two rather than three parts. Kent, understanding Cordelia's deep love for her father and the true natures of Goneril and Regan, tries to dissuade Lear from his 'hideous rashness', but succeeds only in making Lear so furious that he, himself, is banished. When Burgundy hears that Cordelia no longer has a dowry, he refuses to marry her. The King of France, however, who loves Cordelia for herself, takes her to be his Queen.

In soliloquy Edmund reveals that he does not intend to follow the 'plague of custom' by remaining an inferior and '**base**' bastard all his life, but will dispose of his legitimate brother Edgar and seize his father's title for himself. Edmund then convinces Gloucester by means of a forged letter that Edgar is plotting to kill him to inherit all. Pretending loyalty to his brother, Edmund persuades Edgar to flee. When Edgar cannot be found, Gloucester declares him an outlaw and arranges for Edmund to inherit in Edgar's place.

Top ten quotation

At Goneril's castle Lear's behaviour is annoying his daughter. Goneril instructs her steward Oswald to start trouble with Lear's knights so that she may pick a quarrel with her father. Meanwhile, Kent disguises himself as a serving man (Caius) and attaches himself to Lear's retinue, in the hope of protecting the king from the consequences of his folly. Goneril and Lear quarrel bitterly over the conduct of his retainers, and she deprives him of half of them by refusing to pay for their maintenance. Furious, Lear curses her and leaves with his remaining men to stay with Regan. Goneril sends a message to her sister telling her of the quarrel; Regan and Cornwall, keen to avoid Lear's visit, hurriedly leave their castle and ride to Gloucester's.

Kent (as Caius) is sent to Gloucester's castle to prepare the way for Lear's retinue. Kent encounters Oswald and launches a vitriolic tirade against him. When Cornwall and Regan arrive, he continues his diatribe and so is put in the stocks. When Lear arrives to find Caius in the stocks, he refuses to believe Regan could be responsible. An argument between Lear and Regan is interrupted by the arrival of Goneril and Albany. Regan greets her sister warmly and agrees with Goneril that Lear should reduce the number of his retainers. Lear is shocked and hurt to find the sisters united against him. Regan claims he needs no followers at all. Anguished by his daughters' ingratitude, Lear regrets his treatment of Cordelia. Followed only by the faithful Fool and Kent, he exits into a raging storm. Regan and Cornwall bolt the doors behind them.

Dazed by the power of the storm and tormented by his daughters' cruelty, Lear's mind breaks. Kent and the Fool lead him to a hovel, only to find it already occupied by Edgar, disguised as mad Bedlamite 'Poor Tom' to escape the hunt. News of Lear's plight reaches Gloucester, who has secretly determined to help him and who has also learned that Cordelia and France have landed at Dover with an army to reinstate Lear as king. Gloucester confides this news to Edmund, who promptly betrays him to Cornwall and Regan. Gloucester is blinded by Cornwall and Regan but as Cornwall is inflicting this torture a servant intervenes, wounding Cornwall. Regan stabs the servant in the back, killing him; but Cornwall is mortally wounded, leaving Regan a widow.

Learning of Cordelia's arrival, Kent leads the mad Lear to the French camp at Dover. Meanwhile, Edgar finds his blinded father wandering over the desolate countryside. Still pretending to be 'Poor Tom' he leads his father to the Dover cliffs, from which the suicidal Gloucester wants to jump, but Edgar tricks him about where the cliff edge is and so saves his life.

Goneril, contemptuous of Albany's pity for Lear, plots to have her husband killed and to marry Edmund, as soon as they have defeated the French army. Meanwhile, under Cordelia's care, Lear gradually recovers his senses. Urgent matters unexpectedly cause the King of France to return home, leaving his army under the command of Marshal La Far. Just before the battle Oswald encounters Gloucester and tries to kill him but Edgar, now pretending to be a countryman, intervenes. He kills Oswald who, just before he dies, reveals he is carrying letters for Edmund. Edgar reads of Goneril's and Edmund's love affair and of their conspiracy to murder Albany.

Now disguised as a man-at-arms, Edgar gives the intercepted letter to Albany, warning him of Goneril's treachery. Edgar tells Albany that if he wins the battle he must sound a trumpet and a 'champion' will appear, who will prove that what is alleged in the letter is true. Albany resolves to punish both Edmund and Goneril after the battle, stating his intention to restore Lear to the throne.

The French army is vanquished, and Lear and Cordelia fall into Edmund's hands. He sends them to prison with a secret order that they are to be murdered: Cordelia's death is to be made to look like suicide. Regan announces her engagement to Edmund, who it seems has pledged his love to both sisters. Albany accuses Edmund and Goneril of treason, saying that if no one answers the trumpet he will fight Edmund. Regan, ill and in pain, is led to Albany's tent.

Edgar, still disguised, answers the trumpet and defeats Edmund in trial by combat. Albany learns that Edgar has been helping Gloucester who, once he realised that his assistant was his own son, was overwhelmed by the passions of 'joy and grief' and his heart burst, causing his death. Goneril, seeing Edmund's condition, exits agitatedly and Albany orders that someone follow her. With his last breath Edmund sends a messenger to stop the murders of Cordelia and Lear. Shortly afterwards, the bodies of Goneril and Regan are brought in. We learn that Goneril poisoned Regan to remove her as a rival for Edmund's love and then stabbed herself when her crimes were discovered.

Lear carries in Cordelia's corpse: Edmund's message was too late. Lear, again mad and broken by grief, dies. In his madness, however, he seems to believe that he sees Cordelia breathe and come back to life. Thus it could be said that Lear dies happily. Albany arranges for Edgar and Kent to rule 'the gor'd state' of Britain. Kent claims that his dead master is calling him and that he will not live long. The remaining characters leave the stage to the sound of a dead march.

Target your thinking

- How does Shakespeare develop his themes and characters as the drama progresses? (**AO1**)
- What dramatic impact does each of the scenes have on an audience? (**AO2**)

Act I scene 1

TASK

As you read the play, think about what dramatic impact each of the scenes has on an audience. You should keep a scene-by-scene diary to note the dramatic features that Shakespeare uses.

The scene contains three distinct movements. In the first, we are first introduced to two of the three characters of the sub-plot (Gloucester and Edmund), and to Lear's faithful servant, Kent. Lear is about to abdicate and divide the kingdom between Albany and Cornwall. We do not hear that they are married to Goneril and Regan, and there is no mention of Cordelia. Gloucester reveals that Edmund is his illegitimate son and describes the 'good sport' he had enjoyed at his 'making', only a short time after the birth of his legitimate son.

TASK

The great Russian novelist Leo Tolstoy (1828–1910) believed: 'The coarseness of these words of Gloucester is out of place in the mouth of a person intended to represent a noble character' ('Tolstoy on Shakespeare: A critical essay on Shakespeare', 1906). Tolstoy is basing his criticism of Shakespeare on his own assumptions about how noble characters ought to speak. How far do you agree that Tolstoy is expressing the view that characters are more understandable when they are one dimensional?

Build critical skills

Gloucester acknowledges Edmund as his son but also tells Kent that he is going to send him away again. Some critics believe that this 'second banishment' is the cause of Edmund's subsequent behaviour. Samuel Taylor Coleridge ('Coleridge's essays & lectures on Shakespeare: & some other old poets & dramatists', 1907) believed that Edmund was outraged by the light way in which Gloucester had spoken of his mother. You will need to decide what you make of Edmund's motives as the play develops. Therefore it is a good idea to keep a reading diary so you can track your attitudes to Edmund over the course of the play.

Context

Illegitimacy rates were rising during Shakespeare's lifetime and notions of illegitimacy were complex. Officially, English Common Law maintained that illegitimates could not inherit, whereas in Civil Law illegitimates *could* inherit property. Edmund is, strictly speaking, a 'filius nullius', a heraldic-legal term for a 'nothing son' - but is effectively legitimised when Gloucester later banishes Edgar. In richer families illegitimacy was not an insurmountable hurdle.

The second phase of the scene begins with Lear's ceremonial entrance: he is accompanied by all three of his daughters, as well as by Albany and Cornwall, and announces that he intends to divide the kingdom into *three*, proclaiming that the size of each daughter's share will depend on her declaration of love for him. Goneril and Regan provide the required flattery and are rewarded, but Cordelia affirms that she loves her father as her duty dictates and no more. Enraged, Lear instructs her to reconsider but she will not do so and he furiously disowns her, ordering Cordelia's portion to be divided between Goneril and Regan. Kent intervenes but is banished. Lear then summons the Duke of Burgundy and the King of France, who have both been courting Cordelia, and he asks who will now have her without a dowry. Burgundy withdraws but France takes her because Cordelia 'is herself a dowry' (line 243). Everyone but Goneril and Regan leaves the stage, but before Cordelia goes she expresses worry about her father's treatment at her sisters' hands.

In the third movement of the scene Goneril and Regan demonstrate their dissatisfaction, scathingly mocking their father's rashness.

Commentary: Arguably the division of the kingdom is implicitly condemned by Shakespeare, but as Lear is over eighty and has no male heir, it is perhaps natural for him to settle the succession. The virtuous characters never accept the reality of Lear's abdication and regard him as king throughout, perhaps showing their opinion of the scheme's inauthenticity: the ambivalence of Lear's role after the abdication is one of the pivotal points of the Tragedy. The first part of the scene has been in prose, but for the entrance of Lear — engaged on ritual ceremonial abdication — Shakespeare uses verse. Most directors make use of a prop — a map showing Britain divided into three — to show visually Lear's most recent plan; perhaps Goneril is correct when she complains 'how full of changes his age is' (line 290). The idea of a love test is doubtless a symbol of Lear's vanity and contains within it an element of cruelty: he has already decided that the **'third more opulent'** should go to Cordelia, whom he loves most. Goneril and Regan know exactly where they stand in their father's affections.

Build critical skills

Like Desdemona in Shakespeare's *Othello*, Cordelia perceives a 'divided duty'. Many fathers more reasonable than Lear feel a pang when they realise they are no longer first in their daughters' affections – but they do not lose control to the extent shown by Lear, who effectively bastardises Cordelia for giving the incorrect response in the love test.

Top ten quotation

Shakespeare is dramatising a fable, a kind of parable with an obvious moral attached. Lear makes a catastrophic error of judgement – there can be no tragedy without the protagonist's tragic flaw.

A related tragic flaw is Cordelia's; imagine what would have happened if only Cordelia had been tactful and had humoured her father, and had not understated her genuine love. Yet this behaviour is not natural to Cordelia, who will not lie. Kent, who throughout the play directs our responses, sees the truth: 'Thy youngest daughter does not love thee least' (line 153).

How materialistic her sisters are can be seen from the imagery they use to describe their 'love' for their father. Goneril's stress on words of valuation – 'dearer', 'rich', 'rare' – is echoed by Regan. Careful students will note that as with the introduction of the word 'nothing', which will play a prominent role in the rest of the play, Shakespeare introduces the idea of sight in Goneril's claim that her father is 'dearer than eyesight' to her. Regan evidently sees herself as a prize of equal worth to her sister, but the dramatist cleverly introduces the words 'true' and 'sense' into Regan's vocabulary: 'true' is ironic but Regan is a creature of appetite and will be governed by her base senses as the play develops.

TASK

Examiners are not impressed with the argument that Goneril and Regan are virtually the same character, so the careful student will try to see them, despite their many shared acts of neglect and evil, as differentiated characters and not as identikit wicked princesses. As you read the play, make careful notes on the differences between the sisters.

Cordelia has fewer lines than almost any other important character in all of Shakespeare. Her quiet, sad statement that she has '**nothing**' to say is the first of many uses of the word. Her two asides, commenting on her sisters' speeches, are necessary so that the audience is left in no doubt of her motives. She cannot compete in the unnatural auction. She goes on to define her love in a way that would satisfy a reasonable father. She loves: '**According to my bond, no more nor less**' (line 93), with the love and honour properly accorded to parents; but on the brink of betrothal, she cannot say she loves her father *all*.

> Top ten quotation

CRITICAL VIEW

'All happy families are alike; each unhappy family is unhappy in its own way.' (Leo Tolstoy, *Anna Karenina* opening line). Tolstoy, the Russian novelist (1828–1910) who wrote *War and Peace* and many other great works of fiction, argues that Cordelia refuses to quantify her love for Lear 'on purpose to irritate her father'. How far do you agree that Cordelia purposely irritates her father in this scene? What evidence can you find for and against Tolstoy's view? Perhaps Cordelia might have some psychological motivation beyond the need for honesty? Work out why *you* think she refuses to lie.

Lear's fury with Cordelia is caused by bitter disappointment. He had hoped to spend his last years with her — to set his 'rest/On her kind nursery' (lines 123–24). The imagery also suggests a 'second childhood', a premonition of what happens in later Acts. His curse reveals for the first time that the play is set in a pagan world: he swears by Hecate, Jupiter and Apollo, and by making Lear do so the dramatist gave himself greater freedom in dealing with controversial religious issues.

When Lear gives up his power he is utterly dependent on his favoured daughters and on the gratitude of their husbands. Albany is the only one of the four with decent instincts, and he is at first dominated by Goneril.

The love and honour of Kent shows that Lear was not always so foolish as he now appears. Here, and later as Caius, Kent is a model of plain-speaking honesty. He calls the king 'mad' and guilty of 'folly', 'hideous rashness' and 'evil' for his fury. His reward is banishment, and he retorts that he will continue a free man, a truth-teller, in a new country. His farewell speech, commending Cordelia to the gods and reminding Goneril and Regan of their promises, is in rhymed couplets, the formality ringing the importance of their choric function.

The reactions of the rivals for Cordelia's hand to her disownment are carefully delineated. Burgundy puts wealth above love, but France finds his love increased by Cordelia's outcast state. His words have additional resonance because of their echoes of St Paul. France dismisses his rival with one scornful adjective, 'waterish', and twice gives the impartial observer's view of Lear's behaviour: 'strange'. His rhymed verse, like Kent's, has a choric function. So, too, does Cordelia's, 'stood I within his grace/I would prefer him to a better place' (lines 275–76).

In the third movement of this scene Shakespeare reverts to prose. Goneril emerges as the dominant character, with Regan, for the moment, merely agreeing. Regan's proposal to 'further think of it' contrasts with Goneril's determination to act 'i' the heat'. Their lack of filial affection prepares us for the horrors that follow.

The first scene of the play, then, is virtually a prologue. We have been introduced to all the main characters with the exception of Edgar and the Fool. We have been warned of the probable results of Lear's foolishness in banishing Cordelia and Kent, and we have been told of Gloucester's adultery. Chillingly, we see that Goneril and Regan are already plotting to overturn the conditions of Lear's abdication.

Act I scene 2

The soliloquy that opens the scene can be thrillingly shocking for an audience: Edmund boasts of his bastardy.

Edmund produces a forged letter, which he allows his father 'accidentally' to see: the letter purports to be from Edmund's brother Edgar and complains that youngsters should be allowed to come into their inheritance early. Gloucester is

> **Context**
>
> When Cordelia says, 'Time shall unfold what plighted cunning hides,/ Who covert faults, at last with shame derides' (lines 282–83), Shakespeare is utilising the old proverb that truth is the daughter of time, and it is here linked with a verse from the Old Testament (Proverbs 28:13), 'He that hideth his sins, shall not prosper'. The chapter was appointed to be read on St. Stephen's Day (26 December), the day on which *King Lear* was performed before James I in 1606.

fooled instantly and curses Edgar without hearing his side of the story. Edmund says he will arrange a test of his brother's intention, assuring his father that the letter is merely to test Edmund's loyalty to his father. Gloucester superstitiously ascribes these upheavals to heavenly influences, a view that Edmund savagely satirises when his father leaves. Edgar enters; Edmund tells him of Gloucester's fury and Edgar is astonished by his brother's suggestion he should hide and arm himself. He agrees to the Machiavellian Edmund's suggestions as easily as his father did, however. The scene ends with another soliloquy when Edmund tells the audience that, 'if not by birth', he will 'have lands by wit'.

Commentary: The 'Nature' that Edmund addresses with these words: '**Thou, Nature, art my goddess; to thy law/My services are bound**' (lines 1–2) can be seen to be very different from the 'Nature' that Lear later addresses as 'dear goddess' (I.4.267). In *Shakespeare's Doctrine of Nature* (1949), John Danby argues that the virtuous characters in the play look on nature as kindly, whereas the evil characters regard nature as a mere justification for their unscrupulous impulses. It is generally Shakespeare's evil characters who deride the influence of the stars. In *Julius Caesar* it is the envious Cassius, in his temptation of the nobler Brutus, who tells him that the fault 'is not in our stars, but in ourselves'. It is possible to argue with Danby's analysis, however, by analysing the outcomes the dramatist constructs for the characters: whatever the characters' interpretation of it, nature merely exists. Nature does not choose to save those who believe it to be beneficent, nor does it choose to punish those who see it as a conduit through which to channel their own antisocial behaviour. Nature just is: *est* (Latin *it exists*). It is important for you to arrive at your own interpretation of such issues as the role of nature in the play.

Edmund declares in the last line of the scene: 'All with me's meet that I can fashion fit' (line 182): that is, the end justifies the means. Edmund, as his soliloquy makes clear, is determined to rise in the world: and even his love affairs will become subordinated to his ambition.

Top ten quotation

Context

Shakespeare closely follows what he read in Ortensio Lando's *Paradossi* (1543): 'The Bastard is more worthy to be esteemed than he that is lawfully born or legitimate'. Though most editors acknowledge that Shakespeare uses Lando, only a select few acknowledge that Lando was a humorist and that the tract was a series of parodies and amusing paradoxes (*paradossi* in Italian).

Context

Il Principe (The Prince, 1532), a political treatise by Italian Niccolò Macchiavelli (1469-1527), argues that all means may be utilised for the establishment and preservation of authority - 'the end justifies the means' - and that the worst acts of the ruler are justified by the wickedness and treachery of the governed. The Prince, condemned by Pope Clement VIII, is responsible for bringing 'Machiavellian' into usage as a pejorative term.

Edmund's manipulation of Gloucester and Edgar can be comic on stage. With drama, everything depends on the production values of the director and actors. The sub-plot is fictional and entirely Shakespeare's own; it is undoubtedly more contemporary than the main plot. The proverbial 'Nothing will come of nothing' is echoed in Gloucester's quip: 'If it be nothing I shall not need spectacles' (lines 35–36), and reminds us of the frequent imagery connected with sight. The dominant nature of Edmund's character is driven home by Shakespeare's use of drum-like alliterative repetitions of 'd' sounds: 'death', 'dearth', 'dissolutions', 'divisions', 'diffidences', 'dissipation' (lines 145–47).

The view, imputed by Edmund to Edgar, that sons should manage the revenue of aged fathers, echoes what happens in the main plot and it is important that we place this idea in a context. The humane and sophisticated French philosopher Michel de Montaigne remarked in his *Essays* (1580):

> It is mere injustice to see an old, crazed, sinew-shrunken and
> nigh dead father ... to enjoy so many goods as would suffice for
> the preferment and entertainment of many children, and in the
> meanwhile, for want of means, to suffer that to lose their best days
> and years ... a father overburdened with years ... ought willingly to
> distribute ... amongst those, to whom by natural decree they belong.

Context

In his *Essays*, the French philosopher Montaigne (1533-92) reveals disgust at the violence between Catholics and Protestants and questions the place of man in the cosmos, claiming that we do not have good reason to consider ourselves superior to animals and thus arguing against traditional concepts such as the Great Chain of Being (see p.68). In *King Lear* Shakespeare makes full use of Montaigne's philosophy, perhaps best described as a mixture of wise scepticism and humanism.

Context

Although the prediction quoted by Gloucester (lines 103-14) was common enough for the era, it is also similar to the prophecy of the end of the world in the Bible (Mark 13), when 'the brother shall deliver the brother to death, and the father the son, and the children shall rise against their parents, and shall cause them to die ... the sun shall wax dark, and the moon shall not give her light'.

Not everyone in Shakespeare's audience would have thought that to give more power and authority to young people went against Nature.

Act I scene 3

Goneril, after learning of Lear's and his followers' riotous behaviour, instructs her steward Oswald to be disrespectful to Lear. If her father objects, Goneril says he can go to Regan where she is sure he will receive the same sort of treatment; she will write to Regan to arrange that both sisters 'hold' the 'very course'.

Commentary: In this scene the audience first hears the Fool and we are given an insight into Goneril's scheming nature. She will find every opportunity of quarrelling with Lear in order to drive him to Regan, who will continue to humiliate him: Goneril is still planning, ensuring that her will is done. We are given a glimpse into Lear's allegedly wild nature (an active octogenarian, he is even now out hunting) and are intrigued to see if he will behave erratically upon his next appearance. Neither sister, at this point, wants to kill their father; they just want to extricate themselves from the uncomfortable agreement by which they would each have an unwelcome guest and his hundred companions to feed, clothe and house for half the year. Unlike Edmund, who selects his mode of behaviour as an aspect of his free will, Goneril and Regan will gravitate slowly into a sort of depravity that, arguably, becomes far sicker than Edmund's.

Act I scene 4

Kent, now disguised as Caius, has shaved off his beard ('razed my likeness') and altered his accent, thus continuing the theme of disguise and deception. He is hired by Lear: note that Kent's assumed name is not revealed to the audience until the final scene. When Oswald, following Goneril's orders, insults Lear, Kent trips him up. The Fool enters and repeatedly reminds Lear of his great stupidity.

When Lear berates Goneril for her coldness her reply is a resentful rant about his bad behaviour. When she demands a cut in his retinue Lear is enraged, realising his error in banishing Cordelia. Albany protests that he is ignorant of the cause of the disagreement as Lear hurls a terrible curse at Goneril. Lear weeps at the thought that his retinue is to be halved and, imagining better treatment with Regan, storms out. The sympathetic Albany is treated contemptuously by Goneril, who sends a letter to Regan informing her of Lear's behaviour.

Commentary: It is convenient to divide this long scene into four movements:

1 Lear's employment of Kent shows both men at their best: Kent – the personification of loyalty – is still determined to support Lear, who at the outset of the scene is a representative of kingly authority. Lear enters raucously to the sound of horns and demands his dinner, but behaves with initial restraint in the face of provocation: 'I have perceived a most faint neglect of late, which I have rather blamed as mine own jealous curiosity than as a very pretence and purpose of unkindness' (lines 66–69). Oswald's deliberate insolence – the 'weary negligence' (I.3.13) authorised by his mistress – would perhaps have seemed more dreadful then than now, but it annoys Kent, who earns Lear's approval in his new guise. We see the physical violence in the play begin to develop, with Lear striking and Kent tripping Oswald as punishment for his reply of 'My lady's father' (line 77) in response to Lear's question 'Who am I?' This is the first overt denial of Lear's royal authority in the play.

2 During Cordelia's long absence from the stage the Fool acts, as it were, as her representative, never letting Lear – or the audience – forget her. He is the 'wise fool': his resentment at Lear's treatment of Cordelia expresses itself in savage attacks – in songs, in doggerel rhymes and in biting sarcasm. The Fool tells Lear a dozen times that he is a fool, and he will not let him forget his injustice to Cordelia. It is often argued that he is more of a device or cipher than a real, well-rounded character, but his function in holding up a metaphoric mirror to Lear's follies is vital to the play. Tolstoy (1906) unsurprisingly disagreed and hated the Fool, saying of this part of the play:

'thereupon begins a prolonged conversation between the fool and the king, utterly unsuited to the position and serving no purpose. In this manner lengthy conversations go on calling forth in the spectator or reader that wearisome uneasiness which one experiences when listening to jokes which are not witty'. Tolstoy misses the subtlety of the Fool reintroducing the leitmotif of 'nothing', claiming that nothing is what his 'Nuncle' ('mine uncle') has become. The Fool also reminds Lear that he has inverted the natural order of things: 'thou mad'st thy daughters thy mothers' (lines 163–64), and he continues the pattern of savage animal imagery with the violent: 'The hedge-sparrow fed the cuckoo so long/That it's had it head bit off by it young' (lines 206–07).

The Fool introduces the idea of Lear's identity, which results in Lear asking: 'Who is it that can tell me who I am?' (line 221). The Fool's answer – 'Lear's shadow' – underlines how Lear is growing smaller and less significant, and when Lear asks: 'Where are his eyes?' (line 218) the playwright once again links the inability to see with moral blindness. The Fool's comedy is darkly intellectual.

> ## TASK
>
> Continuing his admiration for Hazlitt, the poet John Keats commented in the margin of his copy of *Characters of Shakespeare's Plays*: 'And is it really thus? Or as it has appeared to me? Does not the Fool by his very levity give a finishing touch to the pathos; making what without him would be within our heart-reach, nearly unfathomable?'
>
> What do you think is the importance of the Fool in Act I scene 4?

3   The confrontation between Lear and Goneril is sparked off by Goneril's attitude to the 'all-licensed fool'. Lear, for all his faults, recognises the freedom of the Fool to criticise. The dramatic relationship between king and fool reflects the real relationship between Henry VIII and Will Sommers. That Goneril has no sense of humour is a sign of her egotism, and her attack on the behaviour of Lear's knights is delivered as a Puritan might deplore the behaviour of actors. Such Puritanism is sometimes found in critical opinions. Tolstoy (once again) found the Fool's comedy pointless and unfunny: 'the fool does not cease to interpolate his humourless jokes'. The knights that we do see speak and behave properly, so that Lear's claim that they are 'men of choice and rarest parts' (line 255) may appear to be nearer the truth than Goneril's description of them as 'disordered, so debauched and bold' (line 233). Lear's reactions to Goneril's attack are firstly to pretend that she is not his daughter, then that he has lost his own identity, then again that he does not recognise Goneril or that she is a 'degenerate bastard'. He is not really deluded but the very fact that he is entertaining such possibilities will eventually drive Lear towards madness: we become what we don as costume.

Context

In *Characters of Shakespeare's Plays* (1817), the humanist thinker, essayist and literary critic William Hazlitt (1778-1830) argued that the contrast between Lear's anguish and the petrifying indifference of his daughters would be too painful 'but for the intervention of the Fool, whose well-timed levity comes in to break the continuity of feeling when it can no longer be borne'. Hazlitt is important, because unlike many critics of his time he valued the role of the Fool.

Lear's curse on Goneril, 'Into her womb convey sterility' or, failing that, hoping she has an ungrateful child so that she may feel 'How sharper than a serpent's tooth it is/To have a thankless child' (lines 280–81), is genuinely disturbing. Some actors ascribe Goneril's later savage treatment of Lear to her horror at the curse, claiming it is shocking how much Lear loathes Goneril. Lear's rage at this point has been classified as 'strange and unnatural' (Tolstoy here showing he was occasionally able to see what others saw in *Lear*). Albany enters in time to hear his wife called a 'Detested kite' (line 254) and he stands amazed at the terrible curse. In Lear's mind Goneril is an animal: sea-monster, kite, wolf. Lear promises to tell Albany why he is so enraged but fails to do so in the fourteen lines before his exit. Lear's faculties, like the verse structure Shakespeare uses to convey them, are beginning to fragment.

Context

As the Fool is never on stage with Cordelia, within some modern productions the same actor plays both roles. In Shakespeare's company the Fool was played by Robert Armin, whose previous parts included Feste in *Twelfth Night* - his last song in that play is echoed in III.2. As Armin is not known to have played female parts, the theory that Armin played both parts is to some scholars unlikely. The Cordelia/Fool theory, however, has growing support.

Context

West Country hunchback Will Sommers was Henry VIII's Fool. He was allowed to sit at the royal table, and was even included in official royal portraits. Sommers helped precipitate the downfall of Cardinal Thomas Wolsey by jocularly informing Henry that Wolsey was hoarding gold. One of Henry's only true friends, Sommers called the king his 'uncle' in the phrase 'mine uncle', from which the Fool's name of 'nuncle' for Lear derives.

▲ Henry VIII and his Fool, Will Sommers

4 Albany begins to worry about Goneril's attitude to Lear. She scorns Albany's 'milky gentleness' and his 'harmful mildness' (lines 337 and 340), accusing him of being an effeminate weakling. Goneril's humiliating treatment of her husband is underlined by her calling for Oswald, himself weak and effeminate, and sending him on a confidential mission to Regan. When we next meet Albany (IV.2) he knows that Goneril and Regan have driven their father mad, and soon afterwards that Gloucester has been blinded. He will escape from his subservience to Goneril via his growing realisation of her evil.

Act I scene 5

Lear, waiting impatiently for horses to convey him to Regan, sends Caius ahead to announce his arrival. The Fool taunts Lear about his expectation that Regan will treat him any better than Goneril, but Lear's mind is elsewhere: he fears losing his reason, thus allowing the plot to take on a more psychologically complex nature. The thought of his treatment of Cordelia destabilises him: 'I did her wrong' (line 24), and he is haunted by the spectre of 'monster ingratitude' towards 'so kind a father'.

Commentary: Shakespeare, in fusing the two plots so that Gloucester's fate is linked with Lear's, presumably found it dramatically satisfying to have the success of Edmund's plot against Edgar, and the final humiliation of Lear by Goneril and Regan, take place at Gloucester's castle. The word 'mad' reverberates three times in two lines, grimly prophesying Lear's fate. Audiences will now probably identify with Lear's situation and sympathise with his fear.

Act II scene 1

Curan brings two pieces of news important to the plot: that Cornwall and Regan will be arriving at Gloucester's castle that night and that there is an impending civil war between Albany and Cornwall. Edmund, alert as ever, manipulates both pieces of news, telling Edgar that his hiding place has been discovered and asking him if he has said anything derogatory about Cornwall or Albany. Edmund then persuades Edgar to flee and wounds his own arm, not only to make it appear that Edgar is dangerous but also to earn the gratitude of his father and Cornwall. The superstitious Gloucester, still believing Edmund's tales of Edgar's 'mumbling of wicked charms' and 'conjuring the moon' (line 39), promises death for Edgar and arranges that Edmund will now inherit in his place. Cornwall, when he arrives, confirms Gloucester's sentence on Edgar and takes Edmund into his service. Regan declares that the reason she has unexpectedly visited Gloucester's castle is that she did not want to be at home to welcome Lear and his entourage. Either Goneril has been a successful conspirator in getting Regan to leave her own castle before her father's arrival or Regan is using her sister's advice as a cover for her own bad behaviour, which will become more and more barbaric as the play develops.

Build critical skills

Lear does not know – and nor do we until II.1.58 – that Regan and Cornwall are about to visit Gloucester's castle. Editors assume hopefully that Lear is referring to the town of Gloucester, where Cornwall supposedly resides, but audiences surely are likely to assume that the earl himself is meant. Such minor plot deficiencies probably pass unnoticed in the theatre but are more noticeable when the play is an examination text.

Build critical skills

It is unusual in Shakespeare that a character with a name does not appear again in the play, but this is what happens to Curan: it is possible that the compositor of the Folio misread 'courant' (French for runner, i.e. messenger) as 'Curan'.

Commentary: It perhaps helps to see the impending civil war, which never materialises, as a symbol of the breakdown in law, order and well-managed civilised relationships. Lear's abdication has unleashed the potential for anarchy and, now that there are only two factions (Cordelia's portion would have ensured a balance of power), the audience is aware of political as well as personal rivalries at work. It will become increasingly clear that Cornwall and Albany are distinct characters with very different natures. The audience must decide for themselves whether or not Edmund's reasons for forcing Edgar's escape are believable: some critics argue that it is 'utterly incomprehensible' (Tolstoy) for Edgar to run away on such scant prompting, while others refer to Edmund's psychological power over his half-brother; besides, Edgar is alarmed at the prospect of three potential enemies (Cornwall, Albany, his father) converging on him at the same time, and therefore his panic may well be credible.

For a more detailed analysis of the interplay between Edmund and his brother and father in this scene, please see the 'Analysing texts in detail' section (p.91).

An analysis of the language Edmund employs to address his brother (lines 20–32) reveals that Edgar is verbally assaulted by a bewildering array of questions, dire warnings and instructions. Presumably disoriented and overwhelmed, he manages only one sentence in reply, in the form of a half-line. In this way Shakespeare demonstrates Edmund's superiority of thought, action and speech over Edgar. Gloucester's behaviour may be interpreted as a form of stupidity: his readiness to believe Edmund, who is still hardly known to him, can be seen as foolhardy but Shakespeare has already taken pains to present Gloucester as superstitious and credulous so it can be argued that his behaviour is in character. Gloucester's gullibility at believing his disloyal child's lies and his rashness in seeking a stern punishment for his true child mirrors the character and behaviour of Lear in the main plot and therefore the audience is able to identify thematic links between the different strands of the plot, further developed by Cornwall's and Regan's flight mirroring Lear's flight from Goneril. In terms of the era of composition perhaps the audience should not judge Edgar and Gloucester too harshly: there was a stage convention of good characters believing wicked ones, due in part to the legacy of medieval morality plays based on Christian doctrine that mendacity could not be discovered at the point the deception was enacted. Restorative justice has to wait.

The world has turned upside down for Gloucester in a matter of days; when he wails 'O madam, my old heart is cracked, it's cracked' (line 90) it is both a mournful lament and a reminder of the imagery of cracking, breaking and shattering that infiltrates the entire play. The breakdown in family structure introduced in Act I is continued here: there is painful irony in Edmund's description of Edgar's alleged disloyalty as 'unnatural' and in Cornwall's description of Edmund's 'child-like office' (line 106). Perhaps the most profound irony of all comes in line 84, when Gloucester praises Edmund as his 'Loyal and natural boy'.

Context

The main theme of the highly allegorical morality plays that were popular in medieval and early modern Europe is that man begins in innocence, falls into temptation, repents and is saved. Life, therefore, is a series of trials. The central action is the struggle of man against the seven deadly sins, personified into real characters. The three greatest temptations that man faces are The World, The Flesh and The Devil. 'Sin is inevitable' but 'repentance is always possible'.

Act II scene 2

Kent and Oswald meet in Gloucester's courtyard. Oswald does not recognise Kent, who taunts and beats him. The scuffle is broken up but Kent will not desist and also insults some of the others present. Cornwall, breaching protocol on several levels, has Kent placed in the stocks. Kent protests, supported by Gloucester, but Cornwall remains unmoved. Gloucester remains behind to sympathise with Kent who, when left alone, produces a letter from Cordelia, who has already learned of what is happening to her father and who proposes to help Lear.

Edgar enters, having escaped his pursuers. He tells the audience that he will disguise himself as a lunatic, a wandering Bedlam beggar known as Poor Tom.

Lear is outraged to find Kent in the stocks. Kent reveals Regan's reactions to Lear's letter and how he berated Oswald. Lear goes to fetch Regan but returns furiously when she and Cornwall refuse to see him. When they eventually appear and Kent is freed Lear asks for their sympathy, but Regan promptly supports her sister's stance and suggests that Lear goes back to Goneril with a smaller retinue and apologises: Lear's response is to curse Goneril and her beauty. Goneril herself arrives, which makes Lear even angrier, but the sisters ally to suggest that Lear return with Goneril. Lear still insults Goneril, calling her a diseased corruption. He believes he will be able to stay with his full retinue with Regan, but she swiftly tells him she will not accept even fifty knights. Lear emotionally reminds his daughters of his generosity – 'I gave you all' (line 439) – but Regan upbraids him spitefully: 'in good time you gave it'. The sisters are united. Lear needs no followers whatsoever: not a hundred, not fifty, not even twenty-five, ten or five. Humiliated and fearing the onset of madness Lear leaves the stage, threatening his daughters with curses of revenge but promising that he will not weep in front of them. Gloucester warns Lear's daughters and Cornwall that the old man is preparing to go out into the wild night but they do not care: he has chosen his own course of action and deserves no sympathy.

Build critical skills

Some critics argue that the timescale is out: 'Caius' has been in Lear's service for about a day, which does not allow enough time for an exchange of letters between Britain and France. Others argue, however, that Shakespeare cleverly compresses time for dramatic effect. Does the 'letter' part of the scene add to or diminish your enjoyment?

Context

In Shakespeare's day the size of a retinue, not merely of monarchs but of nobles, was of immense importance. When Elizabeth I visited Kenilworth Castle in July 1575 on one of her Royal Progresses, she arrived with such a vast entourage of people and equipment packed into almost three hundred carts that the host, Robert Dudley, Earl of Leicester, was left nearly bankrupt for the rest of his life. Dudley, 43 at the time, was playing for huge stakes: he hoped to persuade Elizabeth, then 42, to marry him. As a symbolic gesture Dudley arranged for the castle clock to be stopped at the exact time of Elizabeth's arrival to indicate that she had entered a 'magical world' where outside time and reality ceased to matter.

Build critical
skills

Audience
members who
have had
difficulties in
looking after
elderly parents
might express
sympathy for
Goneril's and
Regan's stance
here: Lear
has behaved
foolishly; he still
wants to have
the trappings of
power and he
can undoubtedly
be difficult. What
do you think
Shakespeare
wants the
audience to think
of the sisters'
behaviour at this
point in the play?

Commentary: Kent's invective against Oswald is splendidly funny. It is, however, a serious dramatic moment: Kent is striking a metaphoric and literal blow against the forces of darkness. The oily Oswald is bettered as well as battered by a loyal man, a representative of the old-fashioned virtues under threat in this world of increasing madness and selfishness. Kent's comic outburst reasserts values that most audiences hold dear: he contrasts Goneril with 'the royalty of her father' and candidly admits:

> I have seen better faces in my time
>
> Than stands on any shoulder that I see
>
> Before me at this instant.

(lines 91–93)

Cornwall's true nature emerges in supporting Oswald, insulting Lear's age and clapping Kent in the stocks with no thought for his office as Lear's representative, and we begin to dislike him. This dislike turns to something more potent when he brushes aside Kent's complaints and usurps Gloucester's position in his own household. Shakespeare also begins to add dark shades to Regan's character when she malevolently doubles Kent's punishment. Cruelty without a reason is always frightening. Gloucester's character is also shaded more carefully by the playwright here: coarse and gullible though he has been up to now, we warm to his sympathetic treatment of Kent and are heartened by his attempts to intercede with Cornwall. The letter from Cordelia is difficult to follow. Perhaps Kent is sleepy or the letter is difficult to read by moonlight; perhaps Kent is reading disconnected scraps of the letter or the text is faulty. The intention, however, seems clear enough. Cordelia has been informed of Kent's disguise and is planning to intervene on her father's behalf.

Edgar's speech, in which he states his intention to become 'Poor Tom', is meant to be contemporaneous with Kent being placed in the stocks. Edgar's speech is frenetic and urgent, not only conveying the fact that he has just evaded a manhunt but also giving the audience the first opportunity to see him on his own. It can be argued that here we see him act (as opposed to *re*act) for the first time. The disguise of a mad beggar gives Shakespeare scope for dramatic potentials later in the play: demented ravings, crazy prophesies and gobbledegook about demons make for very effective theatre.

Context

To introduce the theme of poverty into *King Lear* Shakespeare needed a figure at the very bottom of the social scale. Edgar disguised as Tom fills this role. There was a huge depression in Elizabethan England during the 1590s and 1600s. Land enclosures, whereby the rich took control of common land, were progressing rapidly. Even the poor's dwellings were being torn down. Poor Tom represents the desperate, dispossessed rural poor.

On a more complex level, the disguise enables Shakespeare to introduce the theme of 'Unaccommodated man'; Edgar is exposed, vulnerable, almost naked. His pretended madness prepares us for Lear's genuine madness later. The final words of this speech echo the theme of 'nothing', this time in relation to the destruction of self-image and old identity: 'Edgar I nothing am' (line 192).

Shakespeare made excessive use of Samuel Harsnett's *Declaration of Egregious Popish Impostures*, printed in March 1603. Harsnett's pamphlet was printed on the orders of the Privy Council (the formal body of advisers to the king) as part of the ongoing propaganda war against Catholicism. A sceptic over such matters as demonic possession and witchcraft, Harsnett's intentions were to discredit Jesuit priests accused of conducting bogus exorcisms on impressionable females and to draw attention to people who, like Edgar, feigned the symptoms of madness and demonic possession to gain sympathy and money.

There are at least 67 textual echoes of Harsnett's work in *King Lear* (see 'Sources', p.60 of this guide) and Shakespeare was certainly interested in the differences between assumed and genuine madness. People who lost the capacity to reason were considered mad and it will be painful for the audience to see Edgar's pretence in contrast to Lear's genuine insanity.

Up to now the Fool's barbs have been against Lear's folly, but here his critique begins to encompass the selfishness of humanity at large: children are kind to their parents, he suggests, only in self-interest. The poor are always the unluckiest people. When Kent asks why Lear travels with so small a retinue the Fool tells him that he deserves to be stocked for asking such a naive question. Lear's star is waning and only stupid people will follow a fading light. Yet the Fool does not take his own advice and chooses loyalty, giving the audience perhaps the first real glimpse of his depth of character. The audience can now grow to admire him in much the same way as they admire Kent.

For a detailed analysis of the remainder of this scene, please refer to the 'Extended commentary' section on p.92 of this guide.

Tolstoy's résumé of the whole of Act II is: 'Such is the second act, full of unnatural events, and yet more unnatural speeches, absurdly foolish which have no relation to the subject.'

Act III scene 1

Kent meets one of Lear's retinue on the heath. This knight says the king is defying the storm to do its worst. The king's only companion is the Fool, who is jesting to relieve Lear's anguish. Kent reveals the enmity between Cornwall and Albany and that civil war is likely. Cordelia has already been informed of all of this and a French army has landed. Kent sends the gentleman to Dover to inform Cordelia of Lear's suffering.

Commentary: Shakespeare prepares us here for Lear's madness. Another function of the scene is to enable the audience to see that there are cracks in the ranks of Lear's opponents and that Cordelia's help is close at hand. Dover,

A
Declaration of egregi-
ous Popish Impostures, to with-draw the
harts of her Maiesties Subiects from their
allegeance, and from the truth of Christian Religion
professed in England, vnder the pretence of
casting out deuils.

PRACTISED BY EDMVNDS, ALIAS
Weston a Iesuit, and diuers Romish
Priests his wicked associates.

Where-vnto are annexed the Copies of the
Confessions, and Examinations of the parties themselues,
which were pretended to be possessed, and dispossessed,
taken vpon oath before her Maiesties
Commissioners, for causes Eccle-
siasticall.

AT LONDON
Printed by Iames Roberts, dwelling in
Barbican. 1603.

▲ Samuel Harsnett's *Declaration of Egregious Popish Impostures*, printed in March 1603 mentioned here for the first time, is established as a symbol of new hope and redemption. Perhaps most significantly, the storm shows man as battling the elements in the image of Lear striving to 'outscorn/The to and fro conflicting wind and rain' (lines 10–11). Though futile, there is something majestic in his defiance.

Act III scene 2

Lear rails against the elements in between the Fool's jokes. Kent discovers the king and begs him to seek shelter but Lear, who fails to recognise Kent, attacks evil and hypocrisy. Suddenly aware of imminent madness, Lear contemplates the Fool sympathetically and they go off in search of a hovel. The Fool makes a cryptic prophecy before he exits.

Commentary: The old man who stumbled off stage in Act II scene 2 now projects a mad but mystical grandeur, delivered via Shakespeare's verbs of violence: 'blow', 'crack', 'rage', 'spout', 'drenched', 'drowned', 'cleaving', 'singe', 'shaking', 'strike', 'spill', 'rumble', 'spit'. The nouns supplement the effect: 'winds', 'cataracts', 'hurricanoes', 'fires', 'thunderbolts', 'nature', 'fire', 'rain', 'wind'. Adjectives like 'sulphurous', 'executing', 'horrible' and 'foul' intensify the violent mood, and adjectives of age ('white', 'old', 'infirm', 'weak') remind the audience of Lear's advanced years. The cumulative effect is not only that Lear is caught in the worst storm anyone has ever seen but also that he has become a storm of emotions that changes direction with violent ferocity.

There are nightmarish visions wrapped up in the middle of all this: whole churches including steeples and weathervanes underwater; oak trees split asunder; an old man's head being scorched; nature being pillaged of its seed-stock. At first Lear wants to destroy mankind and punish its ingratitude by destroying all future means of germination. Then he tells the 'elements' (the instruments of the gods) that he does not accuse them of 'unkindness' to himself but berates them for being the 'servile ministers' (compliant agents) of his daughters. His next change, upon Kent's arrival, sees him attempting patience but then asking the gods to use the storm to terrify sinners into confessing their wickedness. This is a key change in the scene: Lear is no longer solely obsessed with the ingratitude of his daughters but begins to question sin in general. Significantly, Lear acknowledges his own sin (the first stage in Catholic confession) but claims: '**I am a man/More sinned against than sinning**' (lines 59–60). When he acknowledges the Fool's suffering ('I have one part in my heart/That's sorry yet for thee', lines 72–73) he shows that he is becoming aware of the poor and outcast. He is aware of the foul reality of the lives of the dispossessed, which inspires sympathy. Ironically, now that he is on the edge of madness, he can see things more clearly than when he was king: 'The art of our necessities is strange,/And can make vile things precious' (lines 70–71). This is a profound insight.

Top ten quotation

The Fool's adaptation of the final song in *Twelfth Night* is interesting (lines 74–77): the man like Lear who has 'tiny wit' must be contented with what Fortune throws his way. As a stage trick the song carries a special resonance as it was sung by Robert Armin, who had enjoyed much success in the role of Feste in *Twelfth Night*. By reprising the song the first audiences of *Lear* were as aware of Armin the entertainer as they were of the Fool, thus rendering the anachronistic prophecy spoken by the Fool both timeless and contemporaneous.

The prophecy is not entirely original, being based on George Puttenham's *Art of English Poesie* (1589). Merlin is supposed to have lived some thousand years after Lear and a thousand years before Shakespeare, so the prophecy is still unfulfilled after two thousand years. Tolstoy regarded the Fool's prophecy as 'still more senseless words' and believed they were 'in no wise related to the situation'. The injustice, decline of faith, corruption, sexual mayhem and the many unnatural elements described in the world of *King Lear*, however, were with the audience in the early seventeenth century and arguably are with us still. The effect of the prophecy on stage can be very eerie. The Fool is timeless and he is a potent image from Tarot.

Context

The Fool's prophecy is not in the Quarto, and since most scholars and editors who prefer the Quarto version believe the Folio version was to accommodate theatrical cuts, its presence in all the major editions of *King Lear* is fascinating, puzzling even, as it makes the play fifteen lines longer. Some scholars view it as an addition of Armin's (a clever man, he was certainly capable of writing it), whereas others see Shakespeare as the author.

Context

▲ The Fool's Tarot card

Tarot cards were used across Europe from the mid-fifteenth century and, from the late eighteenth century, have been used by mystics and fortune-tellers for divination. The Fool's Tarot card is the perfect circle, zero, 'nothing'. Egged on by a strange animal symbolising the inner motivations that spur us on, the Fool, with his meagre bundle and pilgrim's staff, is bold enough to explore creation and step towards the unknown, often the edge of a precipice.

Act III scene 3

Gloucester tells Edmund of his distress at the sisters' and Cornwall's cruelty, perturbed that they would not allow him in his own castle to comfort Lear. He confides in Edmund, referring to a letter promising military aid for Lear, and encourages Edmund to keep Cornwall occupied so that his kindness to Lear goes undiscovered. Alone on stage, Edmund promptly reveals that he will betray his father to Cornwall. Thus Edmund knows he will be able to make his father unpopular with the new ruling clique and gain Gloucester's lands and titles.

Commentary: This quiet interlude between two storm scenes shows the further intertwining of the main and sub-plots. Gloucester decides to be loyal to Lear but his fate is sealed when he includes Edmund in his plans. The irony of Gloucester beseeching Edmund to look after himself is painful to behold: Edmund knows that 'The younger rises when the old doth fall' (line 24). Gloucester is truly blind here: 'unnatural dealing' is indeed afoot, and not only in the bosoms of Goneril, Cornwall and Regan.

Act III scene 4

Lear takes shelter in the hovel but ushers in the Fool first, expressing his sympathy for the poor. The Fool rushes out, screaming in terror at encountering Poor Tom, whom he has taken for a spirit. Lear concludes that the naked beggar has been reduced to such a condition by cruel daughters. Fascinated by 'Tom', Lear questions him. Tom's nakedness defines his essential humanity ('**Is man no more than this?**', line 101), so Lear seeks to show fellow-feeling with him by tearing off his own clothes. Gloucester enters and informs the ragged band that he could not bear to obey Lear's 'daughters' hard commands' and has arranged food and shelter. Lear, however, cannot bear to be parted from Tom, his 'noble philosopher', so Tom joins the motley band as they exit towards the shelter.

> Top ten quotation

Commentary: Lear reminds Kent of the relative nature of despair. Great sorrows cancel out small ones and great mental suffering numbs the mind to physical pain. 'When the mind's free/The body's delicate' (lines 11–12) brings to mind both the Middleton and Rowley play *A Fair Quarrel* (1617) and Boethius' *De Consolatione Philosophiae* (c.524). In *A Fair Quarrel* the line ''Tis no prison when the mind is free' appears to be an echo of Lear's line. Boethius' work was an influential text and reflects on how evil can exist in a world created by a benign God and how humans can make themselves happy in a world governed by ever-changing Fortune.

Lear seems to be aware that if he could marshal his mental resources he could yet save himself, but the pain caused by his daughters' 'filial ingratitude' reveals the boundary point through which he enters the realm of madness. The 'madness' gives Lear many wise insights: he prays not to the gods but to the '**Poor naked wretches**' (line 28) whom he ignored when he held power. The idea of sharing society's superfluous wealth will be echoed by Gloucester in

> Top ten quotation

Act IV scene 1, when he gives his purse to Edgar. Both Lear and Gloucester learn that sharing will help undo excess so that everyone can have enough. This fair society, however, can only be brought about by the willed actions of those who have a 'superflux' of wealth. Thus Shakespeare is criticising such things as tax policies that make the rich richer and the poor poorer, or that enclose lands with the result that honest peasants must become beggars or thieves – these were dangerous sentiments in early seventeenth-century England.

For a more detailed analysis of Lear's and Edgar's madness in this scene, please see the 'Analysing texts in detail' section (p.91).

Lear's new understanding prompts his kindness in ushering the Fool in to the hovel before he himself enters. Yet Lear is 'mad' and he assumes that only the unkindness of daughters could have driven Tom mad (lines 48–49, 62–63, 66–67, 69–70). Edgar's madman antics illustrate Shakespeare's brilliance: he mingles bits of doggerel, nonsense, biblical fragments, bawdy, snatches of old poems and snippets of proverbial wisdom. Above all, Shakespeare makes Edgar counterfeit the behaviour of a demoniac, a person possessed by demons, which usually lends an uncanny atmosphere of terror and black magic to the play in performance.

This is a very difficult scene to perform well: we have been forewarned about Edgar's disguise so hopefully will not laugh at Edgar's mad antics (the unfortunate practice in Shakespeare's time was to laugh at 'lunatics'). There are strands of reason in Tom's demented ravings if one looks deep enough.

Much of the horror of the scene lies in the fact that we witness a real lunatic confronting a counterfeit lunatic. Lear gropes for meaning as his understanding breaks down: disease ('plagues') and animal savagery ('pelican daughters') occupy his thoughts; sexuality leads to begetting children who will be cruel. The Fool finds something uncharacteristically sensitive and fearful to say in this new circumstance: 'This cold night will turn us all to fools and madmen' (line 77). When Lear finds in Tom's nakedness an object lesson in what it is to be human (**'Unaccommodated man is no more but such a poor, bare, forked animal as thou art'**, lines 105–6), he tears off his own clothes. How far will the director allow Lear to get: a few buttons? His shirt? All of his clothes? If the poor old man stands naked we are reminded that he has become 'nothing' and of how far he has fallen. Famous naked Lears have included Ian Holm (National Theatre, 1997) and Sir Ian McKellen (Royal Shakespeare Company, 2007–2008).

> Top ten quotation

The light of Gloucester's beacon symbolises safety. He comes to lead his king to shelter and food – basic human needs – yet Lear is so preoccupied with his new-found 'philosopher' that he scarcely notices. Gloucester's presence introduces more painful ironies: he speaks kindly of Kent and reveals that Edgar's supposed plot has 'craz'd his wits', not knowing that both men are present. His words about parenthood – 'Our flesh and blood, my lord, is grown so vile/That it doth hate what it gets' (lines 141–42) – are true of both Gloucester's and Lear's predicaments, though whereas Lear knows Goneril and Regan are responsible for his misery, Gloucester is yet to learn that it is Edmund not Edgar who is responsible for his.

Act III scene 5

Angry to learn that Gloucester is in contact with Cordelia, Cornwall swears revenge and gives Gloucester's titles to Edmund. He then instructs Edmund to seek out his father so he can be arrested.

Commentary: We see here the vindictiveness of Cornwall, contrasted with the kindness of Kent and Gloucester in the previous scene. Again Edmund plays his part brilliantly, pretending that it is a wrench for him to betray his 'blood' and go against his father. Cornwall's promise of fatherly affection is as vile as Edmund's unscrupulous treachery: these two reptiles sicken us but we are still aware that whereas wickedness is in Cornwall's very nature, Edmund has chosen wickedness for policy. It is perhaps a struggle for the audience to decide which manifestation of evil is worse.

Act III scene 6

Preoccupied with vengeance against his daughters, the mad Lear decides they must be arraigned. Despite Kent's attempts to pacify him, Lear is determined to assemble a bench of 'learned justicers' – himself, Tom and the Fool – to try Goneril and Regan. Two stools embody the sisters. Tom and the Fool humour Lear but Edgar is so overwhelmed in doing this that he struggles to continue his counterfeit. Lear eventually sleeps as Gloucester brings news of a plot against the king's life. Gloucester has brought with him a cart in which Lear may be taken to Dover and the safety of Cordelia. Left alone on stage, Edgar has a soliloquy in his own voice.

Commentary: The 'trial' part of this scene is not in the Folio and can be left out on stage to the director's taste. Edgar's soliloquy is also omitted from the Folio version and suffers the same fate in production: sometimes in and at other times out of a performance.

Build critical skills

Some critics claim that the trial scene only encourages the audience to laugh cruelly at lunacy, whereas others such as G.K. Hunter, the editor of the New Penguin edition, claim that the scene weaves 'the obsessive themes of betrayal, demoniac possession, and injustice into the most complex lyric structure in modern drama'. What, in your opinion, is to be gained and what is lost by omitting the trial scene in a theatrical performance? How might changing views towards mental health affect interpretations of this scene?

This scene (typically of *King Lear*) is symbolically important. Movement towards Lear's possible rescue has been shown in his movement from his own castle to Goneril's, to Gloucester's, to the heath, to the hovel and now to Gloucester's outhouse. He has been 'exiled' on the heath – his lowest point thus far – but now is on the road to Dover and the promise of succour. His early exit from the stage in the first scene was in a tempestuous rage, whereas in this scene he is carried off senseless. Yet he still has friends and allies who will risk their lives for him and in such a dark play a little light is welcome. Note how Lear's previous threats of violent punishments for his cruel daughters are now superseded by a desire for justice. In this we can certainly see his madness but can also detect the old king groping towards a society in which the rule of law is important.

The trial is in many ways absurd, and audience reaction to it is steered, as ever, by the quality of the production as well as by the audience's view of the absurd.

The trial – conducted by a lunatic, a counterfeit madman and a Fool – is perhaps Shakespeare's cynical commentary on the reliability of human justice and the legal system. Goneril is tried for her symbolic crime; she 'kicked the poor king her father' (lines 47–48). The startling animal imagery of the play is continued via the reference to Goneril and Regan as 'she foxes' and the demoniac atmosphere is heightened by Tom's gibbering. Perhaps the most alarming image is when Lear requests that Regan be anatomised (her dead body dissected) to see 'what breeds about her heart', asking 'Is there any cause in nature that make these hard hearts?' (lines 73–75). The question is, in one way, a simple one: is she wicked, or merely diseased? Shakespeare extends the dynamic of the debate about the nature of evil to incorporate the question of whether we are made cruel by fate, nature or even God (a dangerous question), or whether we choose cruelty voluntarily as a component of free will. To the fathers in a modern audience, the image of a dead daughter being dissected is probably far more terrifying than Tom's devils.

This scene sees the Fool's final lines in the play: 'And I'll go to bed at noon' (line 82), referring perhaps to his early departure from the play or to his premature death.

Build critical skills

The Fool was unpopular in Restoration productions so he was cut by Nahum Tate in his 1681 adaptation of *King Lear – The History of King Lear* – and not reinstated until 1838 by William Macready who reinstated the use of Shakespeare's original text. More recent criticism has tended to sentimentalise the Fool or view him as the key to the whole play: the intelligent 'outsider', loyal and decent, who represents 'worldly common sense' (George Orwell). In modern literature the character of John Givings in Richard Yates' 1961 novel *Revolutionary Road* is frequently cited as an example of the madman who speaks the truth. In the same way that the Fool understands the concept of nothingness, Givings understands hopelessness. What do you think is lost and gained by the Fool's early departure from the play?

Context

In philosophy 'the absurd' refers to the conflict between the quest to find some meaning to human life and the inability to do so. Absurdists believe that since no meaning is obvious the question is: once individuals become conscious of the absurd, how should they react to it? Suicide, like Gloucester attempts? A religious acceptance of a higher authority, as Kent and Edgar seem to favour? Pessimistic acceptance? Humour?

To see a comic interpretation of absurd justice, visit www.youtube.com/watch?v=SOCBMOfQLc4

Edgar's concluding soliloquy is frequently disliked for its moral tone, which can be judged as out of keeping with the play as a whole. In its favour, it allows the audience to remember the 'real' Edgar, learning as he goes and sensitive to the predicaments of others, making him, perhaps, a worthy king-in-waiting. The rhyming couplets could indicate that the speech should not be taken naturalistically but rather as a choric comment on the action.

Act III scene 7

Cornwall requests that Goneril return to Albany with news of the French invasion. The sisters propose punishments for Gloucester: Regan wants to 'Hang him instantly' but Goneril prefers to 'Pluck out his eyes' (lines 4–5). Cornwall instructs Edmund to accompany Goneril, as what is about to happen is not fit for him to witness. Oswald enters and reports Lear's escape. Gloucester is dragged in, tied to a chair, abused and insulted. Gloucester admits he has helped Lear in order to spare him more cruelty at his daughters' hands and Cornwall blinds him in one eye. As he is about to blind him in the other eye he is stopped by a servant who is sickened by the sadism (Tolstoy couldn't understand why 'some servant for some reason' wants to intervene). They fight, until the good servant is stabbed in the back by Regan. Then Gloucester is blinded in the other eye. Gloucester appeals to his son Edmund for vengeance, but is told that Edmund was responsible for his betrayal. Gloucester now realises that he has wronged Edgar. Discovering that Cornwall has been seriously wounded, Regan helps him from the stage. Two servants remain and pass judgement on the deplorable acts of depravity they have just witnessed, before following Gloucester in an attempt to ease his pain and to secure for him 'the Bedlam beggar' as his guide.

Commentary: This is a truly horrific scene. The sisters' enjoyment of cruelty is transparent and Cornwall's premeditation of the act so sickeningly vile that we are left shaken. We are soon shown that Gloucester has been condemned without trial. Here, as in scene 5, Cornwall talks of revenge rather than of justice, and he admits that what he is about to do is illegal. It is also a terrible violation of hospitality, as Gloucester points out. Regan, whom Lear thought was tender, emerges as cruel and sadistic. The crazed parody of a trial in the previous scene was a model of rational sanity compared to what the audience experiences here. The imagery connected with sight – which Shakespeare utilises from the very first scene in the play to the very last – moves out of metaphor and into horrible fact with Gloucester's blinding.

Realising that he is doomed, Gloucester reveals why he supports Lear:

Because I would not see thy cruel nails

Pluck out his poor old eyes; nor thy fierce sister

In his anointed flesh stick boarish fangs.

(lines 55–57)

Though Goneril is not present for the blinding, it was her idea to pluck out Gloucester's eyes. Regan plays an active part in the gratuitous violence. How Gloucester is blinded on stage will depend on the director: productions have shown Gloucester's eyes kicked out, gouged out ('Out, vile jelly', line 82), trodden on with sharp heels, drilled out with a spike, sucked out, scooped out with a spoon, scoured out with riding spurs, burnt out with a hot poker … Gloucester's first eye is sometimes thrown on stage and stamped on to make sense of the line 'Upon these eyes of thine I'll set my foot' (line 67). When Regan (usually screaming) says 'One side will mock another: th'other too' (line 70) some directors have her joining in the action, putting out Gloucester's other eye herself (with her own nails, a spike, a dagger, a bodkin …) or helping her wounded husband do the deed. Psychopaths have been described as 'morally depraved individuals who represent the "monsters" in our society. They are unstoppable and untreatable predators whose violence is planned, purposeful and guiltless' (see www.cassiopaea.com/cassiopaea/psychopath_2.htm). According to this definition, Cornwall and Regan are certainly psychopaths. In the seventeenth century they would have been seen as the embodiment of evil.

Context

In 2011 Jon Ronson published *The Psychopath Test: A Journey through the Madness Industry*. The book, a bestseller on both sides of the Atlantic, explores the concept of psychopathy, keeping Hare's 20-part Psychopathy Checklist firmly in focus as well as analysing the broader mental health 'industry', including mental health professionals and the mass media. Ronson concludes that as well as certified 'criminals', many corporate and governmental leaders fulfil the criteria to be described as psychopaths.

Many modern productions show Regan enjoying some level of sexual arousal from the depravity, either overtly touching herself intimately or conveying her excitement in a more tacit way, such as via her breathing and facial expressions. Her cruelty is terrifying (no animal is so base) but her jibe 'let him smell/His way to Dover' (lines 92–93) identifies her with the animal sense of smell. The overall effect is grotesque and upsetting. Where does sadism and psychopathy fit in the Great Chain of Being?

We witness vital sparks of human decency in the behaviour of the servant, without which this scene would be a vision of hell unleashed. This remains one of the most harrowing scenes in all theatre.

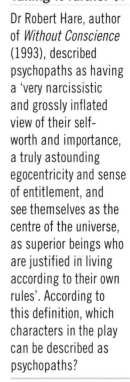

Taking it further ▶

Dr Robert Hare, author of *Without Conscience* (1993), described psychopaths as having a 'very narcissistic and grossly inflated view of their self-worth and importance, a truly astounding egocentricity and sense of entitlement, and see themselves as the centre of the universe, as superior beings who are justified in living according to their own rules'. According to this definition, which characters in the play can be described as psychopaths?

Anna Maxwell Martin ▶
played Regan as a highly
sexualised woman in the
National Theatre's 2014
production directed by
Sam Mendes. This version
of Regan clearly had an
Electra complex

Build critical skills

While some critics
see little of major
significance in
the intervention
of the servant (he
dies; Gloucester
is still blinded),
others argue that
the humanity
and courage of
Cornwall's servant
have far-reaching
consequences:
in this moment of
personal bravery
and rebellion
the humble and
anonymous
servant sets off
a chain reaction
that will lead to
the threatening
of the evil
characters' plans.
How important
do you think this
scene is in terms
of the play as a
whole?

Act IV scene 1

Edgar consoles himself with the thought that, as he is at the lowest point
of Fortune's wheel, things can only get better. At this point Gloucester enters,
led by an old retainer. Gloucester bemoans the folly of his treatment of
Edgar, who in turn acknowledges to himself that there can indeed be further
depths of misery.

Unaware that he is Edgar, Gloucester asks Poor Tom to guide him to Dover. After
arranging for the old man to bring 'the naked fellow' better clothes, Gloucester
gives Tom money as a reward for leading him to the cliff edge, apparently so
that he can end his life there.

Commentary: Confronted with the sight of his father, Edgar confesses that
his circumstances are even worse than he first believed: 'I am worse than e'er
I was' (line 28). This is grim news for the audience: there may be more misery
awaiting us even when we think we can take no more.

Context

▲ The Wheel of Fortune

The Wheel of Fortune (Latin *rota fortunae*) was an established idea to Shakespeare's audience. This illustration shows Boethius, of *De Consolatione* fame, conversing with Lady Fortune, who controls the wheel. Our destinies are tied up in the caprices of Fate. As well as Edgar's reference here, Kent in Act II scene 2 also speaks of it: 'Fortune … once more; turn thy wheel' (line 171). In Act IV scene 7 Lear contrasts his misery on the 'wheel of fire' to Cordelia's 'soul in bliss' (lines 46-47).

Gloucester's admission that 'I stumbled when I saw' (line 21) reveals both to the audience and to Edgar that he is wiser now that he is blind, realising Edgar's innocence and Edmund's guilt. This scene introduces Gloucester's famous couplet about the cruelty of the gods:

> As flies to wanton boys are we to the gods;
>
> They kill us for their sport.

Top ten quotation

(lines 38–39)

Edgar agrees to act as his father's guide to prevent him committing suicide. Tolstoy found such unnatural features irksome, but the symbolic arrangement of the presentation of a blind father (a symbol of humanity) being taught a moral lesson by his saviour (his son), who has not revealed the full mystery of the journey, gives an important metaphoric as well as religious complexion to the scene. That Gloucester's suicide plan involves a 'fall' is, in Christian terms, certainly symbolic of our human condition after the expulsion of Adam and Eve from Paradise. That it will take place at the cliff edge brings the Tarot Fool to mind (see p.21 of this guide).

Shakespeare extracts some powerful ironies from Gloucester's ignorance, as when Edgar uses the ambiguous title of 'father'. For first-time audiences the scene is genuinely suspenseful: will Edgar reveal his true identity? When?

Furthermore, the symbolic importance of the 'madman' leading the blind, of the poor and outcast exemplifying compassion and teaching the lesson of patience and endurance, is both thought-provoking and moving.

Edgar makes one last speech as a demoniac in this scene (lines 59–66). Afterwards, he gradually comes to speak more sanely, and in a more normal voice. Gloucester assumes that Poor Tom's destitution is caused by heaven's plagues and, like Lear in the storm, he prays that the man with superfluous wealth should share it with the poor. These are not the conclusions that the younger Gloucester would have made when he was concerned about the 'good sport' to be enjoyed during copulation, itself a superfluous act in relation to Gloucester's legally and spiritually sanctioned marriage. Wisdom when it finally comes is often dearly bought.

Act IV scene 2

Arriving at Albany's palace, Goneril and Edmund meet Oswald, who reveals Albany's opposition to them. Goneril tells Edmund that her husband is a coward and that she will 'conduct' Albany's 'powers'. Sending Edmund back to Cornwall, Goneril gives him a favour and kisses him, intimating that she will be his if he 'dare venture' on his 'own behalf'. Edmund promises he will be hers even 'in the ranks of death' (line 24). As Goneril looks forward to her sexual consummation with Edmund, Albany enters and launches a fierce and sustained attack on his revolting wife, comparing her to cannibals and 'monsters of the deep' (line 51). Goneril accuses her 'milk-livered' husband of shameful and foolish inactivity: the French have landed and he has done nothing. As they argue, a messenger brings news of Cornwall's death. While Albany is appalled, Goneril now fears that the widowed Regan will be able to have Edmund. She departs to read a letter from Regan; the messenger tells Albany that it was Edmund who betrayed his father to Cornwall and Regan. The scene ends with Albany swearing to 'revenge' Gloucester's eyes.

Commentary: This scene has an important psychological impact. The audience sees a new and dynamic side to Albany, who can now be added to the 'good' characters. His attack on Goneril is a brilliantly sustained piece of invective, which reveals that he is fully aware of her real nature. This is exhilarating and exciting on stage, as we revel in Albany's metamorphosis from comparative nonentity to man of integrity and inner strength. Goneril's vileness is revealed yet further: she is not only an adulterer, but her sexual appetite is rank; she fantasises about performing 'a woman's services' on Edmund, reducing human sexuality to the same level as 'bloodstock beasts'. She is as degenerate a wife as she is a daughter. The dramatic impact is brilliantly sustained in her refusal to budge: she confidently returns the attack on Albany, who warns her that he is tempted to 'dislocate and tear' her 'flesh and bones' and she outfaces him and taunts his manhood. As domestic arguments go, this is a cracker!

Build critical skills

Some critics assume that Goneril's attack on Albany for his 'cowish terror' has some justification, and her patriotic speech (lines 52–59) is regarded as a proper condemnation of Albany's spinelessness. Others argue that Albany's reluctance to fight is not due to physical cowardice but to the doubts he entertains about the right course of action. What is your view of how Shakespeare presents Albany in this scene?

Act IV scene 3

At Dover, Kent meets the gentleman to whom he gave letters for Cordelia in Act III scene 1. We learn that the King of France has been called home, leaving Marshal La Far in charge of the army, and discover Cordelia's tearful response when she is told of her father's suffering. Lear, apparently modulating between bouts of sanity and insanity is, in his lucid moments, too ashamed to see Cordelia on account of the wrongs he has done her. Kent informs the gentleman he will take him to see Lear but that he will remain in disguise for the time being.

Build critical skills

Shakespeare deliberately keeps vague the King of France's reasons for returning home: it was important for the dramatist to show Cordelia's humanitarian rescue mission of her father as lacking any kind of ulterior political motive. What might an audience (in Shakespeare's time and now) make of a French invasion rather than a rescue mission mounted by Cordelia to save her father?

Commentary: Not found at all in the Folio, this scene is included in all major editions of the play, even in Rowse, who breaks his own rule of adopting Q over F. This important little scene reminds the audience of Cordelia. As she has fewer lines than almost any major character in Shakespeare, her entry in the next scene perhaps needs some preparation. The account of her reading the letter about the treatment of Lear by Goneril and Regan accentuates her 'holy' nature. To some critics the description of her tears is sentimental, though stylised and overdone, but to others it forms an essential counterbalance to the violence of the language and actions of the preceding scene.

The scene also highlights Kent's reverential love for Cordelia, maintaining the bond between them, and allows Shakespeare to show the traditionalist Kent's orthodox views on the formation of the human character: '**It is the stars,/The stars above us govern our conditions**' (lines 33–34). Also, the revelation that Lear is so ashamed that he refuses to meet Cordelia prepares the way for their reconciliation later, in Act IV scene 7.

> Top ten quotation

Act IV scene 4

Cordelia, worried by the accounts that Lear is wandering about 'As mad as the vexed sea', sends out a search party for him. The doctor reassures her that he will be able to treat Lear. Learning that the British forces are mobilising, Cordelia states that the only reason she wants to fight is for the 'dear love' and her 'aged father's right' (line 28).

In this scene Cordelia becomes an amalgamation of potent religious symbolism: her association with a beneficent nature ('sustaining corn') gives her a mystical pagan quality. She is deeply Christian too, possessing the purity of the Virgin Mary, bestowing the forgiveness of the merciful Father and using the very words of Jesus. Why do you think Shakespeare takes such pains to portray Cordelia in these overtly religious ways?

Commentary: The scene is a visual spectacle, with the stage directions calling for '*drum and colours*', but the presence of the doctor shows that Cordelia's world is one of caring and nurturing – a far cry from the horrors of her sisters' world. Cordelia's prayer for 'best natural secrets', watered by her tears of love, identifies her with the realms of nature and restorative religion. The comparisons of Cordelia's tears with holy water in the previous scene and the tears of love in this scene combine to give the impression of her natural sanctity, and we are reminded, perhaps, of the Fool's comment about 'court holy-water' in III.2.10. In Cordelia's lines 'O dear father,/It is thy business that I go about' (lines 23–24), Shakespeare clearly intended for an echo to reverberate of Jesus' first recorded words (Luke 2:49): 'Did you not know, that I must be about my father's business?'

Act IV scene 5

Oswald arrives at Gloucester's castle with Goneril's letter for Edmund, who is not yet present. Regan learns that Albany's forces are finally mobilised and says it was a great ignorance letting Gloucester live, as wherever he goes his injuries turn public opinion against her faction. We learn that Edmund has ridden out to assess public opinion and to kill his father if he can find him. Regan, jealous of Goneril's relationship with Edmund, attempts to delay Oswald in order to persuade him to open the letter. He refuses. Regan accuses Goneril of being sexually attracted to Edmund and argues that she, a widow, is better placed to marry Edmund. She gives Oswald a token to pass on to Edmund as a sign of her own sexual and matrimonial interest in him and offers rich rewards to Oswald if he should chance to meet and kill Gloucester.

Commentary: The plot against Gloucester reflects what is happening to Lear in the main plot: Edmund now wants his father dead, mirroring the desire of Goneril and Regan to kill their father. Regan's claim that Edmund is going to kill his father 'in pity of his misery' is vilely hypocritical in the context of the sadistic role she played in Gloucester's blinding. There is something revolting about Regan's desperation to prise the letter out of Oswald's grasp, something pathetic in her revealing her intimate sexual desires to a mere steward, and something sinister in her flirting with a homosexual man and promising 'I'll love thee much' if he does what he is told. For all his faults Oswald remains loyal to Goneril, but when he readily promises to murder Gloucester we are reminded of his poisonous nature. The wicked sisters who have been presented as animals and monsters for so long are finally about to turn their monstrous venom on each other.

Act IV scene 6

Edgar convinces Gloucester that they are climbing the slope leading to Dover cliffs. Gloucester thanks Poor Tom and gives him 'another purse'. After kneeling and claiming it is better to end his anguish now, Gloucester throws himself forward and falls. Edmund now takes on the guise of a bystander on Dover Beach, claiming astonishment that anyone could survive such a prodigious 'fall'. Gloucester is unhappy that in his 'wretchedness' he has been denied the means to end his own life, but Edgar persuades him that he has been preserved by the gods. Gloucester affirms that he has learned a lesson and that henceforth he will bear his affliction until he dies a natural death.

At this point Lear enters, 'crowned with wild flowers' (line 80). He babbles dementedly, but there are moments of lucidity and sense. Gloucester recognises his master's voice and is overcome with emotion: 'O ruined piece of nature' (line 130). Lear eventually recognises Gloucester, telling him 'I remember thine eyes well enough' (line 132). Cordelia's search party enters, but Lear scampers away from them.

Edgar hears that battle is imminent and, as he leads Gloucester to a place of safety, they are discovered by Oswald, who attempts to kill Gloucester. Now assuming the identity of a peasant (with a strange stage accent), Edgar intervenes and fatally wounds Oswald. Before he dies Oswald (loyal as ever to his mistress) beseeches Edgar to deliver Goneril's letter to Edmund. When Edgar reads the letter he discovers Goneril's plot for Edmund to murder Albany. He puts away the letter, intending to show it to Albany. To the sounds of the approaching drums of battle, Edgar leads Gloucester to safety.

Commentary: This scene works best on a symbolic and thematic level. The suicide attempt presents a major challenge in the theatre. The blinding scene is easy to pull off in comparison to the logistics of this: how far should Gloucester fall? Should there be a ramp from which Gloucester jumps? If so, how high should it be? How exactly should Gloucester jump? How should he land? If the production has eschewed naturalism for symbolism and some of these concerns aren't quite so pressing, how can the suicide attempt and its attendant jump be represented symbolically?

Visually, a good production can make the symbolism of the scene work well: Gloucester casting himself over his precipice can have many similarities to the illustration of the Fool in Tarot (see p.21 of this guide), forever frozen in that moment when he is about to leap into the unknown.

The change in Gloucester's mind, from his former position that the gods are 'cruel' to his new view that they are 'ever gentle' (line 213), has been much commented on, especially by critics who want to find some crumbs of comfort in the morality of the play. Edgar's line 'Thy life's a miracle' (line 55) has been cited as evidence of the importance of accepting the Christian orthodoxy, but careful students will remember that after seeing Lear in his madness and being the victim of Oswald's assassination attempt, Gloucester reverts to his pessimistic world-view: 'The King is mad: how stiff is my vile sense/That I stand up and have ingenious feeling/Of my huge sorrows? Better I were distract' (lines 274–76). His change of heart – such as it is – is brought about by pretence: the 'miracle' is a lie, there is no 'fiend'. In human terms Edgar's virtuous deceit for a good end can be said to contrast with Edmund's evil deceit for his own advantage, but both sons lie to their father. In *King Lear* the morality is mercurial.

In Lear's ravings there is a sort of subconscious logic. Ideas crash against each other on the tide of Lear's seaside madness: counterfeiting is coining; coins are

TASK

Most directors do not want to inculcate laughter in the audience in this scene, but how can the director and actors prevent the audience from embarrassed laughter if some of the tricky staging and acting issues are not carefully worked out? Laughter is rare but not completely unheard of here and this can ruin the effect. How would you direct this scene to achieve an effective theatre experience for the audience?

made in a press; soldiers are pressed into service; soldiers practise archery, and so on. In his madness he makes a fierce denunciation of female sexuality ('Down from the waist they are centaurs', lines 121–22). Again Shakespeare has taken some of the sordid details from Harsnett's accounts of exorcisms. Some critics find the comments tasteless: many feminist critics take offence, believing the views expressed are Shakespeare's own. In the theatre the insults shock – as they are intended to – but the audience is aware of their truth at least as they relate to Goneril and Regan and so they carry the weight of revelation.

Mania is often characterised by obsessions with religion and sex. Some of these lines are made into verse in the Folio and editors move between Q and F as their fancies take them. Foakes in the Arden edition of 1997 keeps the speech in verse up to line 120, when he moves to prose with the line: 'The fitchew, nor the soiled horse goes to't …' Some editors imaginatively recreate their own verse between line 120 and 127, but this is a difficult task as the lines cannot be made into any form of regular iambic pentameter. This is perhaps unsurprising, as the lines represent Lear's fragmented and disorderly mind. For an analysis of other important features of the scene, refer to **'Top ten quotations' 8 and 9** on pages 103 and 104 of this guide.

There is a symbolic horror (or is it a dark beauty?) for the audience in viewing Gloucester and Lear – two betrayed and fallen fathers – trying to make sense of their lives. Lear understands he was flattered 'like a dog' (line 97), understands the storm was a pivotal moment and understands the limitations of power: 'they told me I was everything; 'tis a lie – I am not ague-proof' (lines 103–04).

The killing of Oswald perhaps delights the audience: Edgar transmutes yet again – this time into a Robin Hood/Little John sort of figure. He is, after all, still an outlaw. In this guise Edgar's accent is 'Mummerset' (stock stage-yokel; what you might think of as West-Country), which may create opportunities for comedy. A sensitive production, however, can make much of the potential in the scene for an honest son of the soil – as Edgar wishes to portray himself – battering a lick-spittle to death as he attempts an outrageous murder on a blind and defenceless old man.

Oswald ends his life, after being tripped and battered by Kent, with Edgar knocking his brains out. Though the least significant of the villains, Oswald's death and the recovery of the incriminating letter gives the audience some hope that virtue may be rewarded. Edgar has hitherto been portrayed as someone running from confrontation, but now we see him running towards it to become an active agent for the greater good. In a scene of such importance it is symbolically important that we see Edgar – at last – as a genuine man of action.

Act IV scene 7

Cordelia thanks Kent for his great kindness and loyalty to Lear who, dressed in 'fresh garments', is carried on stage. As gentle music plays, Cordelia attempts to wake her father with a kiss. As Lear comes to his senses, Cordelia kneels to greet him in accordance with his full majesty. This is now a humble and lucid

Build critical skills

Tolstoy gets very agitated here: 'the King, after his disconnected utterances, suddenly begins to speak ironically about flatterers … but it is utterly uncalled for in the mouth of Lear. Then Lear declaims a monologue on the unfairness of legal judgment, which is quite out of place in the mouth of the insane Lear.' How do you respond to his views at this point?

Lear, who first thinks Cordelia is a spirit to whom he wants to kneel to ask forgiveness. Acknowledging his folly, age and unsound mind, he recognises the lady who stands before him as his child. Convinced that he deserves her hatred, Lear is prepared to die at Cordelia's hands as atonement for the great wrongs he has done her. Cordelia gently reassures him of her love and, because the doctor has prescribed rest, leads him quietly from the stage.

Build critical skills

The editors Foakes (Arden), Muir (previous Arden edition), Hunter (New Penguin) and Fraser (Signet) all keep in the last section of the scene between Kent and the Gentleman (lines 85–97), which was cut in the Folio. Surprisingly, so does Rowse (Orbis Illustrated), who usually favours Q readings throughout. What in your view does the exchange between Kent and the Gentleman add to the play?

Commentary: This is a serene scene, though Shakespeare places animal references in even Cordelia's mouth: her comment that she would have given shelter to 'Mine enemy's dog' (line 36) echoes Kent's remark that 'if I were your father's dog/You should not use me so' (II.2.132–33), thus maintaining the connection between the characters. The language of this scene is analysed in **'Top ten quotations' 10** on page 104 of this guide.

CRITICAL VIEW

Marianne Novy (in 'Shakespeare and Emotional Distance in the Elizabethan Family', *Theatre Journal*, 1981) suggests that *King Lear* criticises the powerful rights fathers held over their daughters: Lear abuses his authority over Cordelia, and then needs her forgiveness. The balance of the patriarchal structure is subsequently threatened, as the traditional ruler–subject relationship is upset.

Act V scene 1

Regan questions Edmund about his sexual dealings with Goneril. When Albany and Goneril arrive, Albany reveals his mixed feelings: sympathy for Lear and others who have 'just and heavy causes' (line 27) to rebel, but a desire to remove the French invaders. Regan is determined that Edmund and Goneril must not be left alone lest they further their amorous links. Edgar enters in another disguise (this time as a 'poor' but well-meaning stranger) and gives Albany the letter from Goneril to Edmund. He implores Albany to read it before the battle, and if victorious to sound a trumpet whereupon a 'champion' will appear to prove the veracity of the contents of the letter. Edgar leaves and Edmund appears, urging Albany to act swiftly as the enemy is in view; clearly Edmund now considers himself to be – at least – Albany's equal. Albany goes off to battle.

Alone on stage, Edmund reflects on the natures of Goneril and Regan, to both of whom he has sworn his love. He acknowledges that after the battle Goneril will want to kill Albany. The sinister sisters will then try to kill each other, after which he plans to marry the survivor. His motive is self-advancement. He knows Albany will be merciful should he capture Lear and Cordelia, but knowing that their survival will make his chances of becoming undisputed king unlikely, Edmund reveals that he plans to kill them both.

Commentary: With a battle looming and her life in danger Regan, who has grown increasingly neurotic as the play has developed, is obsessed with knowing whether Edmund has had sex with Goneril, and extracts from him a promise that on his 'honour' he has not. Edmund's contempt for Albany is obvious: on stage the line 'Sir, you speak nobly' (line 28) is normally accentuated with a mocking sneer, and the comment 'I shall attend you presently at your tent' (line 34) shows that Edmund will attend him in his own time. Not only is the conflict between Edmund and Albany intensifying, but the rivalry between Goneril and Regan is also becoming manic: Regan interrogates Edmund about his dealings with Goneril three times (lines 6–9, 10–11, 12–13) and is obsessed with the thought of Edmund having found his way to Goneril's 'forfended place' (line 11). Many editors politely gloss this as 'Goneril's bed' but, in keeping with Regan's nature, this is really far more anatomical than that.

When Goneril arrives and notices Edmund and Regan together, she is correspondingly obsessive: 'I had rather lose the battle than that sister/Should loosen him and me' (lines 18–19). The arrival of Edgar builds suspense towards the climax – the audience knows that the letter will confirm Albany's suspicions about Goneril and that Edgar is now prepared to fight Edmund. Following his struggles, Edgar is now a stronger character. Edmund's complete indifference to Goneril and Regan is made startlingly clear: they are pawns in his game; he favours neither. To him they are merely 'these sisters' and both possess the qualities of 'the adder' (line 58). In contrast to their hot lust for him, Edmund is coolly rational about them. Yet this has a sinister corollary: Edmund's rational nature has led him to the conclusion that he must kill Lear and Cordelia if the British should win the battle. The audience holds its breath.

Act V scene 2

Edgar promises to return to Gloucester after the battle but a short time later, following an 'alarum', he returns to reveal that Lear's faction has lost and that Lear and Cordelia have been captured. Gloucester once again gives in to 'ill thoughts', yet again to be talked round by Edgar.

Commentary: The battle is not shown on stage and is conveyed via a stage direction of only four words: '*Alarum and retreat within*', showing that Shakespeare's intention was to represent the action musically, as a retreat was signalled by a trumpet. In a sensitive production much can be made of this opportunity to utilise music. In the History plays Shakespeare's regular practice was to show battles: after *King Lear*, Macduff killed Macbeth on stage, so we are to understand that Shakespeare found compelling reasons for his choice.

Regeneration has been stopped dead in its tracks: Edgar reports to Gloucester that: 'King Lear hath lost, he and his daughter ta'en' (line 6). The audience waits to discover whether Albany's or Edmund's forces have captured Lear and Cordelia, but this is not yet revealed. Gloucester greets the news with despondency but is gently reprimanded by Edgar with a piece of advice that has now become very famous:

> Men must endure
>
> Their going hence even as their coming hither.
>
> Ripeness is all.

(lines 9–11)

The subject of much comment today, in Shakespeare's day this aphorism was a commonplace fusion of the Bible and the service for the burial of the dead in the Anglican prayer book. It also represents a sturdy stoicism recognisable in dozens of books from the period. In his *Essays*, Montaigne claimed: 'To philosophise is to learn to die' and Hamlet, philosophising on death, tells Horatio just before Hamlet's duel with Laertes that 'readiness is all'. It seems that patience and endurance are the human qualities most valuable in the world of *King Lear* and that one of the key concerns for Shakespeare's contemporaries was death and the manner in which one met it.

Act V scene 3

Edmund leads in Lear and Cordelia as his prisoners. Lear longs for imprisonment as it will give him the chance to be with Cordelia, and as they are taken away he defiantly threatens anyone who parts them. Edmund instructs a captain to follow the departed couple and to carry out his written orders – a 'great employment' that 'will not bear question' (lines 33–34) – for which he will receive great reward. The audience realises that this is the order to murder Cordelia and Lear. The captain agrees and departs.

Albany enters and requests that Lear and Cordelia be delivered to him: Edmund explains that they are already in protective custody in case the sight of them inflames the 'common bosom', and are awaiting Albany's judgement. Albany, irritated, informs Edmund that he regards him not as 'a brother' but as a 'subject' (lines 61–62). Regan contests this view and Goneril resents how passionately Regan speaks of Edmund. In the midst of the argument Regan declares that she feels unwell, still claiming Edmund is her 'lord and master' (line 79). When Goneril asks if Regan means to 'enjoy' Edmund, Albany asserts his authority and arrests Edmund ('half-blooded fellow') and Goneril ('gilded serpent') on a charge of treason. Albany orders for a trumpet to be sounded: if no champion arrives to prove the charge he will fight Edmund himself. Regan's illness gets worse and in an aside Goneril reveals that she has poisoned her. Regan is conveyed to Albany's tent. Edgar enters in armour, again unrecognised, and refuses to give his name; he fights and defeats Edmund in single combat. Albany confronts Goneril with the evidence of the incriminating letter but she exits.

> ## Build critical skills
>
> A battle scene would have added drama and excitement but may have made the play longer and made the upcoming duel between Edmund and Edgar rather anticlimactic. Perhaps Shakespeare wanted us to focus on the outcome and not the conduct of the battle. Why do you think we are not shown the battle?

Build critical skills

When Kent enters in search of Lear (line 228), Albany and the others are prompted to remember the king and Cordelia, who have been temporarily forgotten in the confusion and drama. Some critics find this oversight a 'dramatic error', a sign that the demands of plotting had got the better of Shakespeare. Why do you think Shakespeare allows the characters to forget the plight of Lear and Cordelia until this far into the scene?

The dying Edmund admits his guilt. Edgar reveals his identity and recounts how he helped his father, to whom he finally declared himself, but that Gloucester died 'smilingly' overwhelmed by the 'extremes of passion, joy and grief' (line 197). A servant enters carrying a bloody knife and announces that Goneril has committed suicide after confessing to poisoning Regan. Edmund confesses that he has ordered Lear's and Cordelia's execution and an officer is sent to rescind the order and save them. The fatally injured Edmund is carried off.

Lear enters, carrying Cordelia's body. He reveals he killed the officer who hanged his daughter but his anguish is unbearable. When Kent reveals himself, Lear is able to welcome him. Kent tells Lear of the deaths of Regan and Goneril but Lear's mind seems to have turned once again. Albany is then informed of Edmund's death ('a trifle here', line 294) and announces that Lear will be reinstated as king. Lear, however, is in the moment of his final agony. Acknowledging that Cordelia is truly dead and will 'come no more', but then imagining that he can perhaps see her lips move, Lear dies. Albany calls on Kent and Edgar to rule but Kent says he will follow his master to death. The last lines go to Edgar (though the Quarto gives them to Albany), who ends the play with an appeal that we need to speak what we genuinely feel and an acknowledgement that those who survive ('the young') will never see so much nor live so long. The remaining characters leave the stage to the sound of a dead march.

Commentary: Characteristically the final scene of a Tragedy gives the audience the deaths of the protagonist and others, which the genre requires: death, therefore, is the inevitable outcome of the action. There are hints even in this scene, however, that 'all manner of thing should be well', so that the catastrophe when it occurs is heart-rending.

Cordelia's rhyming couplets remind us of both the first scene in the play and of her symbolic significance. They also reveal a woman struggling for control, illustrating her dignity and selflessness. Her request 'Shall we not see these daughters and these sisters?' (line 7) gives the audience an immediate memory of Edmund's categorisation of Goneril and Regan as 'these sisters', only 30 lines previously. The unnatural hags are not worthy even to be named, but to whom is she addressing the remark? Some critics think she is addressing them to Edmund (Hunter in the New Penguin Shakespeare even inserts a stage instruction of his own to convey this), while others (Muir, Penguin *Masterstudies*, 1986) believe she is addressing her father.

Lear, overjoyed at his reconciliation with Cordelia, seems not to know that their time is short and welcomes prison as a paradise where the recognition and forgiveness of his daughter will be repeated continuously. He imagines that he and Cordelia will be able to contemplate the mystery of things such as life, fortune and destiny, and will laugh at all that is shallow. Edmund's harsh and pragmatic instruction 'Take them away' (line 19) shows the realpolitik of the situation and we shudder when he gives the captain his instructions, knowing that his wish to murder Lear and Cordelia is about to be enacted. Lear's next speech (line 20) is mysterious and difficult to interpret: what are the sacrifices on which the gods throw incense? Are they the sacrifices Cordelia has made for her father's sake? Does the remark refer to Lear's and Cordelia's sacrificial deaths at Edmund's hands?

The remainder of Lear's speech is a threat towards anyone who attempts to part him from Cordelia and seems to be a kaleidoscope of jagged Bible stories: 'brand from Heaven' recalls the story of Sodom and Gomorrah (Genesis 19); 'fire us hence like foxes' is akin to the story of Samson and the foxes (Judges 15); Lear's line 'The good years shall devour them' reminds us of Pharaoh's dream of the good and bad years interpreted by Joseph (Genesis 41). No resurrection and life-everlasting here; only firebrands, destruction and death. Not for the first time in the play, Lear claims he will not weep but the audience is really not sure what he means, only that he is in a highly emotional state. In appearance, behaviour and voice he resembles an Old Testament prophet as he is led away.

In the sections that follow, Shakespeare ties up some loose ends from the plot. The action has a tense vigour on stage not always apparent in reading: the audience knows that Goneril's letter is in Albany's possession and we wait to see what Albany will do about it. Furthermore, Regan's announcement that Edmund may take all that is Regan's and 'dispose of them, of me' (line 77) as he wishes, brings the tension of the sex triangle to a climax: Albany arrests Edmund for high treason. In this little vignette we see an unexpected darkly humorous side to Albany's nature: 'If you will marry, make your love to me;/My lady is bespoke' (lines 89–90). Regan meanwhile is beginning to feel the effects of Goneril's poison, which gives a good actor plenty of scope for some physical acting as she is led in agony off stage.

The most physical segment of the scene is of course the duel, which is very medieval in atmosphere and style: three trumpet calls; the accusation of treason and the anonymous challenger are all ritualistic features. Edmund's acceptance of trial by combat can be construed as noble since the rules of chivalry do not require a gentleman to fight an anonymous, masked accuser. The duel itself is (hopefully) a spectacular piece of stagecraft – a metaphor for the struggle between good and evil. Albany's threat to stuff the letter down Goneril's throat provokes her into trying to snatch the letter (a visual echo of when Regan tried to snatch the letter from Oswald in Act IV scene 5), and we witness her complete immorality when she claims that she is beyond the power of justice. How she scurries off stage to commit suicide will depend on actor and director, who can represent her either as a spent force or as defiant to the last, breaking free from Albany's efforts to 'govern her'.

Following the duel the brothers exchange forgiveness, but Edgar's long explanation eats away the time. Audiences generally feel unsettled and uncomfortable at this juncture: Edgar's tale of how he nursed his father before his death and how he revealed his true identity to him takes up some 37 lines and is stopped only by the entrance of the gentleman bearing news of Goneril's suicide.

Context

'Sacrifice' and 'incense' have Judaeo-Christian resonances from Psalm 51 ('Then shalt thou be pleased with the sacrifices of righteousness, with burnt offering … then shall they offer bullocks upon thine altar') and 1 Kings 13 ('upon thee shall he offer the priests of the high places that burn incense upon thee, and men's bones shall be burnt upon thee'). Burnt offerings, dead bullocks and dead men's burnt bones feature in these biblical sources, the nightmarish imagery of which perhaps invades Lear's mind.

Build critical skills

Edgar claims that he led his father to the verge of suicide to save him from 'despair', yet some critics see Edgar as either strange or cruel. S.L. Goldberg (*An Essay on 'King Lear'*, 1974) writes 'Edgar is the most lethal character in the play', accusing him of killing Oswald and Edmund (fair points) but also claiming that he killed Gloucester and drove Lear mad. How do you react to Edgar's account of his 'pilgrimage' here?

More stage time then elapses before Kent's arrival and it is only at this point that the other characters remember Lear and Cordelia. Thus we see how good actions or (as critics who do not approve of Edgar argue) the egocentric self-justifications of our supposedly moral behaviour have no power to stay the hand of evil. Edmund responds to Edgar's account by admitting 'This speech of yours hath moved me,/And shall perchance do good' (lines 198–99), and so the audience anticipates here that he might rescind the order to murder Lear and Cordelia.

Yet Edmund does not interrupt Edgar's account of Kent's last meeting with Gloucester, so tension rises. When the Gentleman crying 'O, she's dead!' (line 223) brings in the bloody knife, we may at first realistically assume that it is Cordelia who has been killed and, when we discover that it is Goneril who has died, we still have hope for Cordelia and Lear. Yet again Edmund says nothing about his royal prisoners, but when the wicked sisters' bodies are brought on stage he finds time to purr 'Yet Edmund was beloved', before he finally arranges for Lear and Cordelia to be saved in line 243. Why does Shakespeare take so long to set the wheels of Lear's and Cordelia's rescue in motion? One answer is to argue that the play is a Tragedy and the deaths are inevitable as theatrical necessities. The delay perfectly heightens the dramatic tension, making the strain almost unbearable. Another view is that the symbolism of thwarted intentions, of good being held in check not necessarily by evil but by human weaknesses of forgetfulness, pride and confusion, needs to be obvious.

Lear carrying in Cordelia's body is the tragic climax of the whole play. Until Nicholas Rowe added the word 'dead' in the stage direction for his 1709 edition, the uncertainty of whether Cordelia is alive or dead added to the tension as Lear's hopes fluctuate. The careful student will notice the number of repeated words and phrases in this section: 'howl', 'stone(s)', 'dead', 'lives', 'gone for ever', 'see', 'straight', 'no', 'life', 'never' and 'look' are all repeated at least twice. The word 'howl' may in fact be a stage direction meant to replicate an anguished animal cry. Albany's prayer that 'The gods defend her' (line 254) is unanswered, as are all prayers in the play. That prayers to pagan gods are unanswered is perhaps unsurprising, but there is more than a hint here that Shakespeare was dubious about the merits of religious belief in general: Kent best sums up the bleak horror of the play in the lines 'Is this the promised end?' (line 261) and 'All's cheerless, dark and deadly' (line 288).

Context

Members of the original audience who had seen or read *King Leir* or who were aware of any of the numerous versions of the Lear story, or knew of the events of the Annesley case (see 'Social context' p.67), knew full well that a happy ending was the usual outcome to this tale. Their shock and horror may therefore have been even greater than that of a modern audience, who expect the tragic outcome.

Yet some critics find a crumb of comfort in the ending. The late-Victorian, highly influential Shakespearian critic, A.C. Bradley (*Shakespearean Tragedy*, 1904) believed that Lear died of joy, thinking he saw a movement of Cordelia's lips. Shakespeare's use of the mirror and feather is masterly. Cordelia and Lear were going to 'sing like birds i'the cage' (line 9). The audience strains to see the tiny feather on stage and waits nervously to see if Cordelia stirs. A reminder of Lear's manly vigour comes in the line 'I killed the slave that was a-hanging thee' (line 272). Lear's line 'And my poor fool is hanged' (line 304) is frequently taken as a reference to the Fool but is perhaps more likely to be a reference to Cordelia: 'fool' was a term of endearment in the early seventeenth century. Yet as Lear grieves for his daughter it is certainly possible that his coxcombed truth-teller is on his mind too.

At the end of the play we may acknowledge that with the deaths of Goneril, Regan and Edmund, evil has been purged. Some critics believe that with the promise of Edgar's rule there is hope for the future, but to many the pain of the ending is too appalling to bear. Why should Cordelia suffer the same fate as her wicked sisters? Where is there any evidence of a benign and comforting deity? Even if good characters have to die at the hands of Evil, where is the promise of heaven for the good?

Samuel Johnson confessed in 1765: 'I was many years ago so shocked by Cordelia's death that I know not whether I ever endured to read again the last scenes of the play till I undertook to revise them as editor.'

King Lear makes us question some of our most profound beliefs about life. If we do not agree with Bradley and Muir that there is some comfort to be derived from the final scene we are forced to conclude that this scene desperately — perhaps madly — tugs at the very fabric of our humanity. Frank Kermode describes the play's 'unsparing cruelty' and the 'almost sadistic attitude to the spectator' (*Shakespeare's Language*, 2000). *King Lear* can be a desperate voyage: the fabric rent asunder in the final scene, as we stare horrified into the nothingness of life; the ragged pages of this bleak text acting as tattered sails blown along on a hurricane of nihilism and absurdism.

CRITICAL VIEW

Again Tolstoy finds no merit in this scene: 'the former coldly pompous, artificial ravings of Lear go on again, destroying the impression which the previous scene might have produced … Lear, although no longer insane, continues to utter the same senseless, inappropriate words'. In particular, Tolstoy dismisses the part of the scene when Lear carries in the dead Cordelia: 'Again begins Lear's awful ravings, at which one feels ashamed as at unsuccessful jokes.' In your opinion, can Tolstoy's view be justified in any way?

Target your thinking

- How does Shakespeare develop his themes as the drama progresses? (**AO1**)
- What dramatic impact does each of the themes have on an audience? (**AO2**)

Nothingness

TASK

As you read the play, think about what dramatic impact each of the themes has on an audience. You should keep a scene-by-scene diary to note the dramatic features that Shakespeare uses.

Lear's exchange with Cordelia on 'nothing' in I.1.87–90 introduces a major theme that echoes down the whole length of the play, via the Fool in I.4.127–30: 'Can you make no use of nothing, nuncle?' and Lear's response: 'Why no, boy; nothing can be made out of nothing', and 'Edgar I nothing am' (II.2.192) to Albany's 'thou art in nothing less/Than I have here proclaimed thee' (V.3.95–96). The word 'nothing' or 'naught' occurs 34 times in the play, showing that Shakespeare is concerned with exploring the idea of nihilism. Regan and Goneril promise much in the beginning, but after whittling down the number of Lear's retainers, they leave him with nothing, and in the end their 'natural' affection comes to nothing as well. His life comes to mean nothing to them as they plot his murder. Lear is progressively brought to nothing, stripped of everything – kingdom, knights, dignity, sanity, clothes, his last loving daughter, and finally life itself.

The growing anarchy of Lear's world is demonstrated in the reduction to nothing of familial and regal bonds. Lear exiles Cordelia and Kent, implying they mean nothing to him. Cordelia's dowry is reduced to nothing. Gloucester believes Edmund, and disinherits Edgar, leaving him with nothing. Yet Cordelia, Kent and Edgar, along with the Fool (number zero in the Tarot – see p.21 of this guide), remain loyal.

The people who have 'all' – Goneril, Regan, Cornwall, and to an extent Edmund – ignore their duties so that wilful greed and self-interest seem to rule the world of the play. 'Nothing' except self-aggrandisement and blatant self-interest is of value to the evil characters, and the good characters' happiness is reduced to nothing. Yet when they are reduced to nothing Lear, Edgar and Gloucester all learn to see the world more clearly and become wiser. Lear sees this in terms of opposites: 'They told me I was everything' (IV.6.103–04). Now he knows better and has become wise by learning that 'nothing' can grow to something. Part of the tragedy is that the chaos is too anarchic to be resolved for Lear, Cordelia and Gloucester. At the end of the play nothing can save them and all is 'cheerless, dark and deadly' (V.3.288).

Nature

The word 'nature' (or its associates such as 'natural' or 'unnatural') occurs 51 times in the text. Quarto 1 is interesting in that it italicises the word 'Nature' in I.4:

> *Leir.* It may be so my Lord, harke *Nature*, heare deere God-desse,
>   suspend thy purpose

It is an interesting slip: as it was the habit of the compositor of Quarto 1 to italicise names, we see that one of *King Lear*'s very first readers regarded Nature almost as a character in the play. In *Shakespeare's Doctrine of Nature* (1949), C.F. Danby argues that Shakespeare presents us with two different versions of Nature: the traditional view that Nature is rational, beneficent and divinely ordered; and the view of the rationalists that man is governed by selfishness and 'appetite'. (See also 'Nature, the cosmos and humankind' on p.68 of this guide.)

Sight

There are an astonishing 135 refers to sight, eyes, looking and blindness in *King Lear*. The references are often used as metaphors for the necessity of sensing potential consequences before embarking on a course of action. The blinding of Gloucester and his subsequent revelation: 'I stumbled when I saw' (IV.1.21) are a more graphical presentation of this idea, which originally appears in Lear's first scene. Goneril declares that to her Lear is 'dearer than eyesight' (I.1.56). Enraged to fury by Kent's intervention, Lear cries: 'Out of my sight!' (I.1.158), only to be reproached with Kent's: 'See better, Lear, and let me still remain/The true blank of thine eye' (I.1.159–60).

Gloucester's physical blindness symbolises the metaphorical blindness that afflicts both Gloucester and the play's other father-figure, Lear. Both have loyal and disloyal children, both are blind to the truth, and both end up banishing their loyal children and making the wicked one(s) their heir(s). Only when Gloucester has lost the use of his eyes and Lear has gone mad does each realise his catastrophic error.

Kent, the Fool and Cordelia show the audience that Lear is more than mere nothing by serving faithfully, speaking bluntly, and loving rationally and according to bond. Although Lear can physically see, he is blind in that he lacks insight. Kent, who has insight, can see through the lies of Goneril and Regan and sees that Cordelia truly loves Lear. Along with Kent, the character least blind and most insightful is the Fool, who sees all with the eyes of a savant. When Lear sees better and is reunited with Cordelia it is a brief respite. No matter how clearly Lear sees now, his earlier moral blindness has set off a chain of consequences that must end in his own destruction. In natural philosophy every action has an equal and opposite reaction: every human action has a consequence. When Edgar says of his father: 'The dark and vicious place where thee he got/Cost him his eyes' (V.3.170–71), the audience is to understand that Edgar is not a sententious moraliser but that he is revealing a bigger, bitter truth about not seeing the future dire consequences of what we do today.

Love and loyalty

Darkness pervades *King Lear*, culminating in the tragic denouement of Act V. Nevertheless, the play presents several central relationships – those between Cordelia and Lear, and between Kent and Lear – as a dramatic embodiment of true, self-sacrificing love. Furthermore, it could be argued that the relationships between Edgar and Gloucester and between the Fool and Lear show how the bonds of love and loyalty can also overcome acts of cruelty, stupidity or neglect. Rather than despising Lear for banishing her, Cordelia remains devoted; Kent never leaves his master's side; the Fool for all his barbs accompanies his 'nuncle'; and Edgar guides and nurses his father into a more optimistic world view. That these efforts succeed only fleetingly gives many spectators some joy; that they exist at all is proof that love and loyalty elevate us above the level of the base and that in our human nature we can have sparks of celestial fire.

Disguise and clothing

There are two main categories of disguise in *King Lear*: the emotional, for example when characters lie, and the physical, when a costume and an assumed identity are worn. Kent and Edgar, who utilise physical disguise, are not motivated by darker emotions but have pure and decent motives. The Fool is also disguised in a sense. Clearly a savant wearing a costume, his supposed 'folly' is wisdom: his 'jokes' truthful reminders of Lear's folly and of Goneril's and Regan's cruelty. Goneril, Regan, Edmund and Cornwall, however, hide their true natures.

Top ten quotation

No matter how clearly Lear comes to see this – **'Through tattered clothes great vices do appear;/Robes and furred gowns hide all'** (IV.6.154–61) – his earlier moral blindness has set off a chain of consequences that must end in his own destruction.

Marxist critics find in Shakespeare's clothing imagery a savage satire on aristocratic manners and affectations. Lear sees through Regan's finery: 'Thou art a lady;/If only to go warm were gorgeous,/Why, nature needs not what thou gorgeous wear'st,/Which scarcely keeps thee warm' (II.2.456–59). Edgar in Tom's near-nakedness is the opposite of aristocratic fashion. The blanket that he wears, 'else we had been all shamed' (III.4.64–65), seems to protect him well enough in the storm. Shakespeare, perhaps following Bovelles' philosophy (see p.71 of this guide), presents a general respect for the common individual: the disguised Kent's service is of the kind 'which ordinary men are fit for' (I.4.34). In the new order, an ordinary man is more valuable than a banished aristocrat. In a similar way, the 'poor naked fellow' Tom guides Gloucester, the blinded aristocrat who needs the commoner to help him 'see'. In Tom's ravings lurks some wisdom: 'obey thy parents, keep thy word justly, swear not, commit not with man's sworn spouse, set not thy sweet-heart on proud array' (III.4.78–80). The naked Tom helps Lear to see the naked truth; Lear says to him: '**Thou ow'st the worm no silk, the beast no hide, the sheep no wool, the cat no perfume**' (III.4.101–03).

Top ten quotation

Wishing to emulate the truth embodied in his 'philosopher's' nakedness, the king begins to 'unbutton'. Previously, Lear has identified clothes with superficial pomp. Undressed, Lear is now like Tom, a free man in a 'state of nature'. Edgar helps Lear to unmask the uselessness of royalty, which is a 'lending' both unnecessary and 'superfluous'.

Target your thinking

- How does Shakespeare develop his characters as the drama progresses? (**AO1**)
- How can a thorough understanding of the play's characterisation extend your knowledge of the text? It is useful to remember that Shakespeare uses his characters to present themes to the audience. (**AO1** and **AO2**)

Lear

Lear's unnatural public testing of his daughters' love demonstrates that at the outset of the drama he values the display of love over real love. Perhaps he is insecure and vain, but there is nothing inherently mad or particularly unwise in longing for retirement at eighty years old. He has no male heirs; perhaps he really believes that future strife may be avoided if he settles the affairs of the kingdom. In wishing to cling to the trappings of power that he has ceremoniously renounced he is guilty of naivety, valuing the illusion of power over substance. He already has the map pre-divided, so the love-test is a court ritual until Cordelia makes it a real family crisis by refusing to cheapen her emotions by auctioning them. Goneril's accusation that Lear is changeable due to his age is possibly true: France twice comments that his casting off of Cordelia is 'strange'. Lear's dragon-like wrath, a measure of his disappointment in Cordelia, sets events in motion that will end horrifically. Rage will exert a terrible price but will turn on itself.

TASK

Despite his folly, of which critics (and the Fool) make much, we should remember that Lear is confronted by serious adversaries. His antagonists are some of the fiercest and most wicked in Shakespeare: Goneril, Regan, Cornwall and Edmund are a vile quartet. How far do you agree that Lear's 'hideous rashness' gradually begins to look less shocking in contrast to the dark crimes and sadistic murders of the evil characters?

▲ Monument to Joseph Stalin in Stalin's birthplace, Gori. In the 2014 National Theatre performance of *King Lear* a very similar monument to Lear featured as part of the scenery. Consider why the director chose to do this and what this could imply

Audiences need to ask whether Lear develops as a character – whether he learns from his mistakes and becomes a better and more insightful human being. His values do change over the course of the play. As early as l.5.24 he realises of Cordelia: 'I did her wrong'; his affection for the Fool is genuine; at times he prays for patience and tries to control his temper. In his mad state he develops some insights into the world that he could not have made when he was a cossetted king: he wishes he had taken better care of the poor naked wretches who live on the edges of society. In his realisation that human life is essentially tragic, that nothingness is in the very nature of things, the audience may even grow to love him as a tortured Everyman as much as Cordelia and his loyal friends have loved him as a father and a king.

When he seeks to kneel to Cordelia, his humility is as genuinely touching, as is her forgiveness. His confession that he is a 'very foolish, fond old man' proves his humanity and self-awareness. As he comes to love his child Cordelia above everything else, we realise that he cannot keep her because the brutal forces his folly has unleashed cannot bear to have love in the world. The vain tyrant of Act I has evolved into a simple man, a loving father who – tragically briefly – loves well and sees clearly. Lear does not die a happy man, but perhaps the audience can take some comfort from the fact that he dies a better man.

Lear's journey is a complex and painful one and the part is a challenge for even the most accomplished actor. To see an interesting photo gallery of actors performing the role, visit the telegraph online and for an insight into how Simon Russell Beale prepared for and acted the role of King Lear, visit YouTube (full weblinks are provided on pp.105–6).

Goneril

Lear's selfish, manipulative daughter justifies her every action and can brook no opposition on anything. She professes great love for Lear: 'Sir, I do love you more than word can wield the matter,/Dearer than eyesight' (I.1.55–56). Yet, once she has taken possession of half his kingdom (nominally that of her husband, Albany), she reneges on her obligation to look after her father and seeks to control him, forcing Lear to comment: 'How sharper than a serpent's tooth it is/ To have a thankless child' (I.4.280–81). As the play develops, so grows Goneril's selfish quest for power. Always a bully, this would-be adulteress becomes a murderer when she poisons her sister. A good actor can elicit moments of sympathy from the audience, which can create complex emotions in the theatre; Kate Fleetwood's 2014 performance portrayed Goneril as 'tense' and 'ruthless'.

Regan

Regan claims that she is 'made of that self mettle as my sister', adding that 'I profess/Myself an enemy to all other joys/Which the most precious square of sense possesses … In your dear highness' love' (I.1.69–76). Early in the play she is content to let the domineering Goneril run the plan to deprive Lear of his retinue and may well be judged to be of the 'self mettle' as her sister. Shakespeare, however, gradually turns Regan from being merely spiteful,

Build critical skills

William R. Elton in 'King Lear' and the Gods (1966) believes Goneril and Regan to be typical Renaissance pagans, possessing an intense preoccupation with the natural and with the self: they are therefore Machiavellian. What do you think is gained and lost by making the audience view the sisters as both rational ('natural') and self-consciously self-serving ('Machiavellian')?

hypocritical and ambitious into a sexual sadist capable of encouraging and possibly assisting in the blinding of Gloucester. Regan's desire for Edmund leads to Goneril fearing then hating her. Eventually her lust leads to her death.

Cordelia

By refusing to take part in Lear's love test, Cordelia establishes herself as a model of sensible virtue. Some critics claim her perfection makes it difficult for an audience to like her, but she is best understood symbolically. For the middle section of the play, she is off-stage, taking on the significance, perhaps, of a female version of King Arthur, who according to legend would return to Britain in the hour of its darkest need. Cordelia's beauty is presented in religious terms and she becomes a sacrifice to the dark, selfish forces represented by Edmund.

Cordelia is not a particularly demanding part for a competent actor to play: in the theatre the actor's size in relation to the strength of the actor playing Lear is as much an issue as anything else – Lear is usually played by an older actor and he has to carry Cordelia on stage in Act V scene 3. The first thing Simon Russell Beale did when meeting Olivia Vinall at the National Theatre's fiftieth birthday celebration was to pick her up to see if he could carry her easily: 'We hadn't been introduced but I had just got the part of Cordelia. He came over and lifted me off the ground. He has to do that in the play and wanted to see how heavy I was. A bit embarrassing.'

To see and hear Kate Fleetwood's, Anna Maxwell Martin's and Olivia Vinall's observations of playing the sisters in *King Lear*, visit YouTube (a full weblink is provided on p.106).

provided on p.106).

▲ King Lear with his daughters (from left): Goneril (Kate Fleetwood), Regan (Anna Maxwell Martin), Cordelia (Olivia Vinall) and Lear (Simon Russell Beale), from the 2014 National Theatre production

Build critical skills

Regan is a demanding role. By modern definitions Regan is clearly psychotic; a weak actor may give in to the temptation to cackle, scream and touch herself up through Acts III to V, which can ruin the effect in the theatre. Anna Maxwell Martin's Regan was described by Charles Spencer of the *Telegraph* as 'A sex kitten turned on by torture' in a 'terrific' performance. How far do you agree that Regan needs to be not only disturbed but disturbing: an example of what we may become if we allow the beast within us to rise unchecked?

Gloucester

To play Gloucester asks a lot of an actor. He has to be glib about the 'sport' he had when making Edmund, and superstitious and gullible enough to believe that Edgar is guilty of planning to kill him. These are unpleasant qualities. Between these scenes, however, he is concerned about Kent's banishment, acknowledging that Kent is 'noble and true-hearted', and is worried about Lear's reduction in power. Thus he has some redeeming features. As the play develops so Gloucester's moral integrity grows. Cornwall has usurped Gloucester's authority in his own castle, but at considerable personal risk Gloucester complains about the stocking of Caius and goes out into the storm to find Lear: 'If I die for it – as no less is threatened me – the King my old master must be relieved' (III.3.17–18). His fatal mistake is in entrusting this information to his son Edmund, who promptly tells Cornwall. This in turn leads to Gloucester's blinding.

Despite his terror Gloucester displays remarkable courage in denouncing Goneril and Regan. His desperation leads to his desire to commit suicide and the scenes that follow demand a great deal of the actor: Gloucester wavers from believing that the gods are conscienceless pranksters who 'sport' (there's that word again) with human life, to believing that the deities are 'ever-gentle'. He has to perform the jump that isn't a jump and convince the audience that he believes he has been preserved by a 'miracle'. Even after this key point in the play his mood oscillates between stoicism and despair. When he meets the mad Lear on Dover Beach, Gloucester's emotions waver between pity and envy. His final appearance in the play in Act V scene 2 is when he is for the final time talked out of despondency after hearing Edgar's 'Ripeness is all' speech: his final words 'And that's true too' (V.2.11) suggest that he has at last accepted stoicism over despair. Gloucester, with the demands of mood shifts, physical acting and fluctuations of perspective, is a challenging role.

Context

Edgar's aphorism that 'Men must endure/Their going hence even as their coming hither./ Ripeness is all' (V.2.9-11) is a compendium of several of Montaigne's observations, including 'To philosophise is to learn to die' and a comment on why the length of our lives is unimportant: life 'consists not in the number of years, but in your will, that you have lived long enough'.

Edgar

Edgar begins as a credulous character but by the end of the play is nominated king. Edgar's progress from gull to king is not to the taste of all critics, who sometimes see him as a simple dramatic device. Edgar is the most disguised character in Shakespeare: a bedlamite; a witness to Gloucester's 'fall'; a rustic defender of Gloucester against Oswald; a chivalric champion in the duel against Edmund: 'His various roles do not tell us more about Edgar. They tell us more about the play in which he is a character' (Leo Kirschbaum, *Character and Characterisation in Shakespeare*, 1962). Other critics disagree, seeing Edgar as a fully developed and unusually sensitive man who feels others' anguish as keenly as his own: 'The various roles he plays are the means by which he matures into royalty' (Kenneth Muir, *Penguin Masterstudies: King Lear*, 1986). Whether or not *King Lear* works as a stage play is as dependent upon the abilities of the actor playing Edgar as on the abilities of the actor playing Lear. Kirschbaum's Edgar is too gullible and too diffuse to comprehend and a bad actor can only reinforce

TASK

Compare and contrast Shakespeare's presentation of Edmund and Edgar. You may wish to consider such things as disguise, ambition, honesty, treachery, sibling rivalry, attitudes to Gloucester, sexuality, Shakespeare's use of soliloquy, and the brothers' very different fates at the play's conclusion.

this view for an audience. Most modern productions strive to show Edgar's developing maturity, but for an actor successfully to project a sense of Edgar's evolution within his component disguises is a demanding challenge, and only very accomplished actors can pull it off.

Edmund

Much is written about Edmund elsewhere in this guide. Edmund is initially popular with the audience and retains devilish charm to the end: he is clever, humorous, handsome, dashing and sexually attractive. An actor has great fun with Edmund, one of the 'plum' roles in the play. In truth, once the director has selected a sufficiently roguish and sexy young man for the part it is difficult to make a bad job of Edmund if the actor is at least competent. For an insight into Sam Troughton's performance as Edmund in the 2014 National Theatre production (as well as Stephen Boxer's Gloucester and Tom Brooke's Edgar), visit YouTube (a full weblink is provided on p.106).

Kent

'See better, Lear, and let me still remain/The true blank of thine eye' (I.1.159–60). Kent, in adopting the disguise of Caius, represents the kind of loyalty that transcends circumstances: as a symbol of undying devotion, Kent's importance in the play is huge. The audience admires 'good Kent' from the outset for his courage and robust morality. Because he is loyal to Lear's 'authority' he helps the audience shape its response to Lear. His end is poignant: he wants to reveal himself to Lear to be acknowledged and recognised for his unswerving support. Some critics argue that Lear scarcely notices him, which seems odd as Lear clearly says: 'Are you not Kent?' (V.3.280) and when Kent asks about Caius, Lear replies 'He's a good fellow'. Much depends on Lear's response to Kent's admission that he and Caius are one and the same: Lear says 'I'll see that straight' (V.3.285), which is usually glossed as something like 'I'll attend to that in a minute', but if Lear means that he'll see it straight in the sense of putting it right then he does acknowledge Kent's contribution, even in the midst of his misery over Cordelia. As usual the play's meaning will be revealed on stage.

Fool

The Fool intensifies Lear's misery by using his sharp wit, but does so to lead the king to acknowledge the sternest truths. Jan Kott, in *Shakespeare Our Contemporary* (1974) says:

> *The Fool does not follow any ideology. He rejects all appearances, of law, justice, moral order. He sees brute force, cruelty and lust. He has no illusions and does not seek consolation in the existence of natural or supernatural order, which provides for the punishment of evil and the reward of good. Lear, insisting on his fictitious majesty, seems ridiculous to him … But the Fool does not desert his ridiculous, degraded king, and accompanies him on his way to madness. The Fool knows that the only true madness is to recognise this world as rational.*

The Fool is a mystical character and to work best the part should be given to an actor who can combine the earthy with the ethereal, the robust with the vulnerable, and the physical with the intellectual.

For an insight into how Stanley Townsend played Kent in the 2014 National Theatre production and how Adrian Scarborough played the Fool, please visit YouTube (a full weblink is provided on p.106).

Cornwall

Regan's husband is characterised by Gloucester as 'fiery' and as the play develops his cruel nature expands: he endorses Goneril's humiliation of her father and it is he who orders that the doors be 'shut up' against Lear and his two companions at the end of Act II scene 2. He enlists the support of Edmund and premeditates, then enjoys, torturing Gloucester. It can be difficult for the actor not to turn Cornwall into a pantomime villain: a good actor, however, will structure his performance so that Cornwall's descent into hell is gradual. The blinding scene needs to be terrifying, so the actor must be able to convey genuine menace.

Albany

Goneril's husband makes a neat counterpoint to Cornwall. When the play begins the two dukes are presented as largely indistinguishable – consorts to the devious princesses, they do little more than decorate the stage in the abdication scene. Yet Albany gradually realises that Goneril is wicked. At first he mildly admonishes her treatment of Lear and is scorned (as he is throughout) for his gentleness. He is off stage for all of Acts II and III, and when we next meet him he is a much more dynamic character, denouncing Goneril's wickedness with a moral authority we did not know he had. The rumour of the civil war demonstrates that he has distanced himself from Cornwall and his belief that if the gods do not intervene to punish human depravity people will eat each other like 'monsters of the deep' shows a firmly held and considered moral view. His realisation that his wife is a compound of 'vile filths' gives the audience hope that the evil characters can be stopped. Towards the end of the play he shows bravery, modesty and decency. There is a long-standing belief in the theatre that Shakespeare himself played the part of Albany at the Globe and before the King and his Court at Whitehall on Boxing Day 1606.

King of France

France, who appears only in the first scene, represents the natural view of Cordelia: 'She is herself a dowry' (I.1.243) and Lear's behaviour: 'Gods, gods! 'Tis strange' (I.1.256). He is noble and selfless, perhaps an unusual presentation of a French King in Renaissance English drama, where the French were often vilified as arrogant, effete or as the 'natural enemy'.

Context

Kent's insults imply homosexuality as something that is considered unnatural. An interesting noun is 'varlet', which appears in both Quarto and Folio versions of *King Lear*: 'What a brazen-faced varlet art thou' (II.2.27). 'Varlet' as a term of abuse for homosexuals occurs many times in Shakespeare's plays – most notably in *Troilus and Cressida* (1602) and *Measure for Measure* (1604), both written around the time of *Lear*'s composition.

Duke of Burgundy

In refusing to continue his interest in Cordelia when he learns that she has no dowry, 'waterish' Burgundy represents political self-interest that is incapable of seeing a deeper moral good. He is a selfish aristocratic nonentity.

Oswald

In Quarto 1, Oswald is called a '*gentleman*' in Act I scene 3 and a '*steward*' in Act I scene 4. By the Folio version, Oswald is referred to as a '*steward*' in each scene and is the brunt of several insults, such as 'whoreson dog', 'slave' and 'cur', and this is common to both formats.

In Act II scene 2 we see Oswald as the object of a sustained verbal assault when Kent recognises him from their encounter when he tripped him up. Some modern directors make much of the line 'Prithee, if thou lov'st me, tell me' (II.2.6) and cast Oswald as a predatory homosexual to justify Kent's unpleasantness. Shakespeare's audience would need no such excuse to dislike Oswald, who is a time-serving lickspittle who has publicly insulted the king. To Kent, he deserved a cuff and a kick.

Oswald's function is that of a spineless manservant to a woman, and perhaps Shakespeare presents him as a homosexual in the eyes of other characters to denote his unmanliness. His death in Act IV scene 6 serves also to highlight Edgar's bravery, which contrasts with Oswald's cowardly nature. Oswald is one of the play's 'unnatural' characters.

Actors' insight

www.telegraph.co.uk/culture/culturepicturegalleries/10595202/King-Lear-in-pictures.html?frame=2800724 –This page shows us an interesting photo gallery of actors playing King Lear.

www.youtube.com/watch?v=xgXM0b6PaHw –Simon Russell Beale on King Lear.

www.youtube.com/watch?v=IV7KFy8I39w –Kate Fleetwood, Anna Maxwell Martin and Olivia Vinall on playing the sisters in King Lear.

www.youtube.com/watch?v=rJzGUqIgB0M –Sam Troughton's performance as Edmund (as well as Stephen Boxer's Gloucester and Tom Brooke's Edgar).

www.youtube.com/watch?v=MhgIhN_3mMk –Insight into how Stanley Townsend played Kent and how Adrian Scarborough played the Fool.

Writer's methods: Form, structure and language

Target your thinking

- Track which language features, such as image clusters, Shakespeare gives to the characters as the play develops. (**AO2**)
- Keep a record of the dominant imagery of each scene (i.e. animals, nothingness, sight and blindness, disguise, lying, honesty, religion, rebellion, violence, madness, etc.) and track how Shakespeare makes each character link to the imagery. (**AO2**)

The genre of *King Lear* is drama and to understand the play it is imperative that you have a sense of it being performed in front of an audience and that you take an interest in dramatic features such as soliloquy, asides, disguise, music, entrances, exits and in which characters are on or off stage at key moments. It is never helpful for students' examination prospects to view drama as an alternative to a prose work such as a novel. It is, however, hugely helpful to arrive at an understanding that the play is a script and that on stage it can be interpreted and presented in a wide variety of ways. Production values are essential in drama as they will set the seal on what the director wants to present as key meanings. Many features of the form, structure and language of *King Lear* are explored further in the 'Scene summaries and commentaries' (p.6) and in the exemplar essays on page 77.

Form

King Lear is a Tragedy, designed as a series of poetic dramatic episodes, which follow Lear's tragic error. Aristotle (384–322 BCE) laid down the template for Tragedy as the depiction of the downfall of a noble person, usually through some combination of *hubris* (overbearing pride; arrogant assumption), fate, and the will of the gods. The tragic hero's desire to achieve some goal inevitably encounters limits – usually those of human frailty, the gods or nature. Aristotle argues that the tragic hero should have a flaw and/or make some mistake (*hamartia*). The hero need not necessarily die at the end, but he must undergo a change in fortune. In addition, the tragic hero may achieve some revelation or recognition (*anagnorisis* – 'knowing again') about the human condition. Aristotle terms this sort of recognition 'a change from ignorance to awareness of a bond of love or hate'.

In these terms King Lear's fate parallels that of Aristotle's classical model. The end of the Tragedy is a catharsis (purgation, cleansing) of the tragic emotions of pity and fear. 'Catharsis' is a term that has generated considerable debate.

<aside>

TASK

Shakespeare's four great Tragedies are *Hamlet*, *King Lear*, *Othello* and *Macbeth*. Unlike the intellectual Hamlet, whose fatal flaw is indecision, the heroes of the Tragedies that followed are undone by catastrophic errors of judgement. Compare and contrast the presentation of madness in these great Tragedies.

</aside>

The word means 'purging', and Aristotle employs a medical metaphor – Tragedy arouses the emotions of pity and fear in order to purge away their excess, to reduce these passions to a healthy, balanced proportion. Aristotle also talks of the 'pleasure' that is proper to Tragedy, meaning the aesthetic pleasure one gets from contemplating the pity and fear that are aroused through an intricately constructed work of art. Tragedy is superior to History in Aristotle's opinion because whereas History can reveal only what *has* happened, Tragedy is concerned with what *may* happen. Thus Tragedy deals with universal truths and History only with specific ones.

Structure

King Lear's plot structure is frequently characterised as complex, largely due to the many parallels between the main and sub-plot (see below). The careful student should note that there are dangers in seeing the two plots as separate lines of action: the different strands are carefully threaded together. The audience can see that what happens to Lear is not a grotesque aberration of nature that afflicts Lear alone, because similarly dreadful things happen to Gloucester. The play explores the darker forces that afflict our *common* humanity.

- Both plots revolve around an elderly father and his adult children.
- Lear and Gloucester both lack judgement and cannot see through selfishness and lies.
- Both fathers are deluded by false children and cast out the good.
- In their turn both men are cast out and have to live beyond civilisation in open nature.
- Both fear madness, though only Lear is afflicted.
- Both men are, at different times, accompanied by Edgar in disguise and are finally accompanied by him together.
- Both men suffer agonies (Lear's is mental; Gloucester's is physical), which lead them to admit that they have abused and wronged a good child: Cordelia and Edgar, respectively.
- Both men undergo a process of renewal and begin to 'see' more clearly.
- Lear and Gloucester are both saved and restored by the child who they had abused and cast out.
- Both men die in similar circumstances, of emotional shock concerning the wronged child.
- Both plots explore sibling rivalry – between sisters in the main plot and between brothers in the sub-plot.

Taking it further ▶

In Tennessee Williams' play *Cat on a Hot Tin Roof* (1955), Edward Bond's play *Lear* (1971) and Jane Smiley's novel *A Thousand Acres* (1991), the writers all follow the narrative thread of Shakespeare's *King Lear*.

Compare and contrast the texts in relationship to ideas concerning, for example, sexuality. In *A Thousand Acres* Larry (Lear) has sexually abused Ginny (Goneril) and Rose (Regan); in *Cat* Maggie has not had sex with her husband Brick for a long time and Brick has turned to drink due to his relationship with ex pro-footballer Skipper, who committed suicide. In Bond's *Lear* Fontanelle is 'bitterly disappointed' in her husband Cornwall and conspires to have him murdered so she can be with Warrington, an Edmund figure.

The relationship between power and lies is also important in all three texts.

Language

As we have already seen in the commentaries on individual scenes, *King Lear* is a play rich in imagery. Repeated references to 'nothing', 'nature', 'daughters', 'sight' and the human 'heart' resonate through the entire play, as do images of suffering, anguish and torment. An analysis of the language of a play will reveal a great deal about its themes, so the careful student will adduce that, by beginning with language and working out towards *King Lear*'s wider concerns, a great deal can be learned about Shakespeare's network of ideas. This includes ideas about nihilism; about human nature and the nature of love; about sight, not only in the literal sense, but as it relates to wisdom and understanding; about fathers and daughters; and about human behaviour, in particular as it relates to the debate on free will and fate.

Early in the play the imagery resonates with references to dragons and monsters, before it settles into a concerted and startlingly thorough image sequence of animals: there are 143 direct references to 67 different animals and approximately 15 indirect references to beasts, creatures or monsters. There are further faint echoes of animal imagery in the play, where Goneril complains that Lear's knights 'carp' or the Fool, talking of apples, uses the term 'crab'.

In all there are 34 mentions of dogs, 19 references to horses, 14 references to different types of birds, eight monsters, six wolves, six bears, five foxes, four snakes, four sheep, three rats, three beasts, two worms, two hogs/swine, two cuckoos, and two creatures. The impact in *Lear* is that the nature of humanity is being continuously measured against the nature of animals. In this sense the play can be seen as an exploration of man's place within the Great Chain of Being and how we can become reduced to the status of animals if we lack sufficient wisdom and self-control.

Taking it further ▶

For the evidence of this multitude of references to animals, see the table presented in the online materials that accompany this guide.

Modern 'eco-criticism' has taken an interest in the play: Simon Estok sees 'ecophobia', or contempt for the natural world, informing Shakespeare's vision and Steve Mentz claims that the play 'mocks human faith in an orderly universe', with the storm at its heart representing 'disequilibrium', the instability that is fundamental to natural systems. Modern understanding of climate change gives this notion added force.

Shakespeare gives Lear a vast array of images. Early in the play he seems preoccupied with his own status as a man who is both loved as a father and feared as the human embodiment of a wrathful dragon. When Lear is angry, Shakespeare puts into his mouth some chilling insults and curses, calling Goneril a 'degenerate bastard', a 'sea-monster' and a 'detested kite'. Some of his insults to Goneril take on a form akin to black magic spells and are shockingly anatomical: 'Into her womb convey sterility,/Dry up in her the organs of increase' (I.4.270–71); 'Infect her beauty,/You fen-sucked fogs, drawn by the powerful sun/To fall and blister!' (II.2.355–57); 'thou art … a disease that's in my flesh … a boil,/A plague sore or embossed carbuncle' (II.2.410–13).

Later, Lear's language modifies as his life changes: he attempts 'patience' several times and Shakespeare reflects his changing psychology by giving him in Act III a style of speaking that is both judicial and religious. It is here that Lear becomes mad: is Shakespeare arguing that it is madness to attempt to construct a meaningful reality based on law and religion? Shakespeare is subtle here: though the world is ostensibly a pagan one, Lear's mind reverberates with Christian images: 'steeples', 'guilt', 'sin' and 'sinning', 'praying', 'the heavens' and 'mercy' are all on his lips in Act III. By Act IV, in the height of his madness when he is obsessed with money, soldiers, adultery and copulation, he still speaks of 'divinity', the 'fiend', 'hell', 'darkness', the 'sulphurous pit', 'beadles', and 'preaching'. When he regains his sanity and recognises Cordelia he speaks of her 'soul' and as she requests 'benediction' he prays she does not weep. A detailed analysis of Lear's biblical references from early in Act V scene 3 is given in the commentary on this scene (p.37), including such words as 'blessings', 'kneel', 'forgiveness', 'pray' and even 'God's'.

Build critical skills

In both Quarto and Folio there is no punctuation on the word 'Gods'. Muir in his Arden edition supplies the apostrophe thus: Gods', keeping what he believes to be the pagan setting, but Foakes' later Arden edition, Fraser's Signet and Hunter's New Penguin provide the apostrophe thus: God's, making their preference for a monotheistic Judaeo–Christian analysis clear. How much potential meaning in one little apostrophe!

Lear's language is intriguing, scalding, scolding and exciting, so it is puzzling that Tolstoy could believe it to be 'characterless'.

Target your thinking

- Try to work out what your own ideal production of *King Lear* would be like based on productions you have seen or read about, either in this guide or elsewhere. (**AO1** and **AO5**)
- How can analysing King Lear within a broad range of contexts deepen your understanding of the text and the ways in which different readers might respond to it? To help you with this analysis you should keep a record of what different theories have been put forward about the play and how different audiences have or may have responded to the play since Shakespeare's time. You will find some ideas in this guide but you should also conduct your own independent research. (**AO3**)

This section is designed to offer you insight into the influence of some significant contexts within which *King Lear* was written and has been performed. You will need to 'demonstrate understanding of the significance and influence of the contexts in which literary texts are written and received'. Such contextual material should, however, be used with caution. Reference to contexts is valuable only when it genuinely informs a reading of the text. Contextual material that is clumsily introduced or 'bolted on' to an argument will contribute very little to the argument.

Biographical context

There are many biographies of Shakespeare, the best of which is Samuel Schoenbaum's *William Shakespeare: A Documentary Life* (Oxford, 1975). Schoenbaum's book is a treasure-chest of documentary evidence and data for every stage and facet of Shakespeare's life. It is a magnificent repudiation of the assertions of the de Vere Society and of others who deny Shakespeare's authorship of the plays.

Context

Some interest groups deny that William Shakespeare of Stratford wrote the plays that carry his name. Snobbery is a motive for this denial: how, is the cry, could a bumpkin with a vulgar father and no university education possibly write such works of eternal genius? These elitist groups favour instead such candidates as Edward de Vere, 17th Earl of Oxford, Christopher Marlowe, William Stanley, 6th Earl of Derby, or Francis Bacon. For a flavour of this heady right-wing moonshine visit: www.deveresociety.co.uk

Shakespeare's life and *King Lear*

❚ In 1568 Shakespeare's father John became Stratford's town mayor ('High Bailiff') and applied for a coat of arms. For reasons unknown, he did not proceed with this application, but the playwright went to pains to win the awarding of the title 'gentleman' and its attendant coat of arms in 1596. There is perhaps a punning reference to this in *King Lear*, when the Fool in Act III scene 6 jokes that 'he's a mad yeoman that sees his son a gentleman before him' (lines 13–14).

❚ One of Shakespeare's brothers was called Edmund.

❚ When Shakespeare married Anne Hathaway in November 1582 she was three or four months pregnant. A special licence was necessary, for there were 'closed' seasons of marriage, unless huge fees were paid. If the couple had not acquired the licence when they did, they would have had to wait until April 1583, by which time Anne would be due to give birth. In terms of King Lear it could be said that in his own life Shakespeare had taken steps to ensure that his own child was not born illegitimate. Shakespeare's marriage to Anne Hathaway was not carried out in Holy Trinity Stratford but was conducted by John Frith in Temple Grafton, about four miles away. Frith was identified in 1586 as a Roman Catholic priest even though he had 'outwardly affected Protestant ways'. It appears that the betrothed couple (literally) went out of their way to secure Frith's services at their marriage.

❚ *King Lear* is a play deeply concerned with religious ideas concerning man's place in the universe, free will and the role of the gods (or God?) in human life. Shakespeare's father and mother were both Catholics, as were their immediate and extended families and several of Shakespeare's teachers at the King's New School in Stratford. Simon Hunt, who taught him for the first four years of his education, went to the Collegium Anglicum (the English Jesuit College) in Douai in 1575. In 1579 Shakespeare's new teacher was John Cottam (aka Cottom), younger brother of the Jesuit priest and Catholic missionary Thomas Cottam, who resided at Douai with Simon Hunt. Here they were joined by Robert Debdale (or Dibdale), a fellow pupil of Shakespeare's and a neighbour of Shakespeare's mother's family in Shottery. Upon their return to England both Thomas Cottam and Debdale were arrested and executed. Both Shakespeare's father and his daughter Susanna were fined for their refusal to attend Protestant services (a crime known as recusancy), and it has been thus inferred that Shakespeare himself was a Catholic. Yale University includes this statement in its 2014 prospectus: 'If students are to understand religion during Shakespeare's life, they must understand that the playwright was probably brought up in a Roman Catholic household in a time of official suspicion and persecution of recusancy.'

❚ In 2009 the Venerable English College in Rome placed copies of their Pilgrims' Book into an exhibition called *Non Angli sed Angeli* ('Not English but Angels'), a title based on Pope Gregory I's quip when he saw English slave boys in the market in Rome some time between 590 and 604. 'Gulielmus Clerkue Stratfordiensis' (*William the scholar from Stratford*) signed the book in 1589; at the time of this alleged visit to Rome, Shakespeare would have been 25. The signature may of course be that of another contemporaneous Stratford scholar named William, but the find is an extremely important one. Schoenbaum, writing before this discovery, argues that one may not prove the Catholicism of a man just because his mother, father and one of his daughters can be proved to be Catholics. Schoenbaum further argues that due to the difficulties for a public figure to be openly Catholic (Shakespeare's friend Ben Jonson got into serious trouble for his open avowal of the Old Faith), as well as other clues such as Shakespeare's knowledge of the Geneva Bible and the baptism of his children and his own burial at the Protestant Holy Trinity Church in Stratford, the likelihood is that Shakespeare was probably a 'tolerant Anglican'. The historian and novelist Peter Ackroyd, also not having access to the newly discovered documents, makes a judgement on the balance of evidence: Shakespeare from his Catholic family with his Catholic friends was obviously a Catholic sympathiser: 'He was, you might say, one of the fraternity.'

How will this debate about theology help you in your study of *King Lear*? You need to be aware that scholars frequently disagree about Shakespeare's intentions. Any position – as long as you can support it with evidence – is valid. To study English Literature is to be a citizen in the Democracy of Ideas. Perhaps Shakespeare was more interested in the dramatic revelation and discussion of controversial ideas than he was in giving his audience yet another set of dogmatic paradigms. Theatre is entertainment with philosophical and moral grace-notes. As ever with A-level, the careful student will begin with the text, then will discover as much as possible about the different competing theories and will make up his or her own mind. Then the student will apply what he or she has learned back to the text.

Historical context

Variant texts of Quartos and the Folio

In Shakespeare's time books were made in various sizes. The two sizes that have a bearing on Shakespearean scholarship regarding *King Lear* are the Quarto and the Folio. A *folio* is a volume consisting of sheets that have been folded only once, each sheet thus making two leaves or four pages; a *quarto* is so called because each sheet of paper has been folded twice, making four leaves or eight pages. Beneath this size was an *octavo*, where each sheet was folded three times, making eight leaves or sixteen pages. Folios were more expensive than quartos; octavos were the least expensive, often being used to produce pamphlets.

The first *King Lear* Quarto (Q1) of 1608 is known as the 'Pied Bull' Quarto due to the bookseller Nathaniel Butter's sign being a pied bull. Twelve copies of this survive, but ten of these are in different states as proofreading

Build critical skills

In 1609 and 1610 a group of Catholic actors performed *King Lear* in various sympathetic houses in Yorkshire. Why do you think the play was popular with Catholic anti-Reformationists and struck some important chords with audiences interested in ideas of the sacred clashing with the secular?

was simultaneous with printing; therefore as early as Q1 textual problems plague *King Lear*. There are 167 individual anomalies within the ten differing versions of Q1.

In the Folio (F) of 1623, *King Lear* takes up pages 283 to 309 and is a copy of Q1 in which certain corrections have been made. In the Folio the title is given as *The Tragedy of King Lear*. The Folio leaves out about 300 lines that appear in the Quarto versions, but then again it adds about 110 new lines not found in the Quarto.

So, what exactly do we mean by the *text* of this play?

Most modern editors jumble up Q1 and F to their own tastes. For instance, in his Arden Shakespeare edition of *King Lear* in 1997, R.A. Foakes generally prefers F; but Kenneth Muir, in 1964 his predecessor as Arden editor, shows many preferences for Q1, though even Muir gives the final speech of the play to Edgar, which is in F. In Q1 this speech is attributed to Albany.

What you see is what you get with *Lear*, the play is a textual minefield. There is no need to worry unduly over such matters as Q and F variants as an A-level student, but conscientious students can impress examiners if they are aware of some of the interesting Q and F variations and use their knowledge to access the Assessment Objectives. For example, most modern editors retain the Q ending to Act III scene 7, which is not found in F; this shows the remaining two servants commenting on the cruelty of Regan and Cornwall after they have blinded Gloucester. G.K. Hunter (New Penguin) and Russell Fraser (Signet), as well as Foakes, however, opt for the F ending of Act V. Only A.L. Rowse (Orbis Illustrated) is consistent in his preference for Q and allocates the concluding lines to Albany. Good students may well be able to make something of these interesting but diverse interpretations of the text of *King Lear*. For example, an informed candidate will impress the examiner by arguing that the discussion between the servants mentioned above (III.7.98–106), which is in Q but not in F, reinforces the audience's hope in a restorative humanity after the sadism of Cornwall and Regan. In terms of AO5 it may also help students to identify Rowse as a consistent and authoritative critical voice.

Date

It is likely that *King Lear* was written in 1606, though it is possible that it may have been slightly earlier. Its first recorded performance was at Court on 26 December 1606, but it had probably been acted at the Globe a little time before then.

Sources

The True Chronicle History of King Leir was published in 1605 and an unsuccessful *Leir* was performed in April 1594 at the Rose by a combined Queen's/Sussex Men. Authorship of *Leir* is anonymous, and unsurprisingly Tolstoy liked it better than Shakespeare's version. There really is no accounting for taste.

Shakespeare makes great use of Samuel Harsnett's *A Declaration of Egregious Popish Impostures* (1603), especially in creating the mad persona of Edgar as Poor Tom.

Harsnett's pamphlet was printed on the orders of the Privy Council as part of the ongoing propaganda war against Catholicism. A sceptic over such matters as demonic possession and witchcraft, Harsnett's intentions were to discredit Jesuit priests accused of conducting bogus exorcisms on impressionable females and to draw attention to people who, like Edgar, feigned the symptoms of madness and demonic possession to gain sympathy and money. The Gunpowder Plot had whipped up a considerable anti-Catholic sentiment in England, which the government wished to exploit further, so Harsnett's pamphlet dredged up allegations from twenty years earlier to keep the pot boiling. As chaplain to the Bishop of London, Harsnett had to read plays in his role as censor. It is highly likely that Shakespeare knew of Harsnett in this capacity, but of further interest is the fact that among the wicked and 'Egregious Popish Imposters' mentioned are Shakespeare's school-fellow Robert Debdale and Thomas Cottam, brother of the John Cottam who had taught in Stratford Free School between 1579 and 1582 (see 'Shakespeare's life and *King Lear*', p.58). Thomas Cottam was executed in 1582; Debdale, suffering the same fate, was hanged, drawn and quartered at Tyburn in 1586. Pope John Paul II conferred the status of 'Blessed' (the last stage prior to sainthood) on Debdale on 22 November 1987. Cottam had been beatified earlier, by Pope Leo XIII on 29 December 1886.

As English martyrs to Catholics, Cottam and Debdale were dangerous and superstitious malefactors to Harsnett, who takes racy delight in describing the gruesome and sexually sordid details of the exorcisms allegedly practised on the possessed by Catholic clergy. Much of Edgar's Poor Tom babble of Frateretto, Flibbertigibbet, Hoppedance, Smulkin, Modu, Mohu, the Prince of Darkness and the Foul Fiend is taken directly from Harsnett. Kenneth Muir finds some 82 direct links to Harsnett in the play (appendix to Arden Shakespeare, 1972). It says a great deal of Shakespeare's mind that he could remember and assimilate material from so many sources.

The influence on Shakespeare of Montaigne's *Essays* was also considerable: G.C. Taylor in *Shakespeare's Debt to Montaigne* (1925) records 23 passages that echo Montaigne and lists 116 words not found in Shakespeare's vocabulary before 1603 that are found in Florio's translation of Montaigne: a list of 96 words coined by Florio when he translated Montaigne is given in Muir's Arden Shakespeare.

In many passages of his *Apology for Raymond de Sebonde* Montaigne (himself a Catholic, though a sceptical one) exposes the weakness of 'unaccommodated man', advising that the rejection of 'ancient custom' – borrowed by Shakespeare for Edmund – will become more widespread with the rise of Protestantism. Montaigne shows his hatred for human pride (hubris) and considers the influence of the stars on human behaviour. Perhaps most importantly of all he writes:

Context

Samuel Harsnett (1561–1631) was a Church of England careerist. He worked hard to discredit and persecute Catholics and Puritans alike. Harsnett discredited Catholics because they hated the idea of a Reformed Church and the new 'made-up' religion of Protestantism, and he attacked the sombre and often extreme Puritans who did not think the Reforms went far enough. Harsnett eventually became Archbishop of York in 1629.

The weakness of our judgements helps us more than our strength … and our blindness more than our clear-sighted eyes.

The impact of Montaigne on *King Lear* is beyond doubt.

King Leir and Shakespeare's *King Lear*

In the *King Leir* of 1605 (see 'Sources', p.60), the dramatis personae are:

- Leir
- Cordella
- Gonorill
- Ragan
- Perillus (Kent in Shakespeare)
- Mumford (a bluff lord who serves Gallia, with some similarities to Kent as Caius)
- Skalliger (a time-server like Edward Bond's Old Counsellor in *Lear*, 1971)
- King of Gallia (who marries Cordella)
- Cornwall (husband to Ragan)
- Cambria (husband to Gonorill)

In the Q1 (1608) and F (1623) versions of Shakespeare's *King Lear* the dramatis personae are:

- Lear
- Cordelia
- Goneril
- Regan
- Kent
- France
- Cornwall
- Albany
- Gloucester
- Edmund
- Edgar
- Fool

The 1605 play is about a straightforward civil war between Cornwall and Cambria that is quelled by the King of Gallia, who reinstates Leir. Cordella (Cordelia) does not die.

So, Shakespeare totally invents the Fool; the whole Gloucester sub-plot (including the heath scene, eye-gouging, *et al.*); the whole 'bastard' motif; and the eventual deaths of both Lear and Cordelia. For Lear's descent into madness he did have a source: see the notes on the Annesley case in 'Social context' below. Though Shakespeare's adaptations and manipulation of other sources reveal his capacious reading and quicksilver skills of alchemical synthesis, perhaps it is in the playwright's pure inventions that we can see the true mark of his genius.

Performance context

Stage history

The Stationers' Register of 26 November 1607 reports that *King Lear* was 'played before the King's Majesty at Whitehall upon St. Stephen's night at Christmas last.' In all probability it had been performed several times at the Globe a little while before its 1606 Boxing Day performance. By analysing the composition of the King's Men in 1606 it is possible to deduce that in all likelihood Richard Burbage played King Lear, Robert Armin played the Fool, and it is probable that John Hemmings acted the part of Gloucester and that Shakespeare himself played Albany. Within theatrical circles there is a long-established legend that the parts of the Fool and Cordelia were doubled – a common enough practice at the time – and were therefore both played by Armin. Lear seems to confuse Cordelia with the Fool on line 304 of Act 5 scene 3: 'And my poor fool is hanged', so we do have some textual authority for the interpretation.

It is possible that the play was slightly modified by Shakespeare for a revival at the Blackfriars indoor theatre in 1609: the putative revision has often been put forward as a reason for the differences between the 1608 Quarto and the 1623 Folio. (See p.59 for a fuller account of the differences between the 1608 'Pied Bull' Quartos and the 1623 Folio.)

King Lear was revived by William Davenant (1606–68) in 1664 and performed to Shakespeare's original Quarto or Folio versions. Davenant is an interesting figure. He is often put forward as Shakespeare's illegitimate son or his real godson, or both. Two years after the playwright's death, in 1618 the twelve-year-old Davenant wrote a poem *In Remembrance of Master Shakespeare*, which he published in 1638. Shakespeare does seem to have had a connection to Davenant and his parents, who ran the Crown Inn in Oxford, a convenient overnight stop-over on the road from Stratford to London.

As an adult Davenant was a staunch Royalist during the Civil War but after the Battle of Naseby in 1645 he fled to France, where he converted to Roman Catholicism. After an adventurous life, which included being captured at sea, imprisonment in the Tower of London and writing the Heroic poem *Gondibert*, his fortunes reversed when Charles II was restored to the throne. Davenant profited from the re-opening of the theatres, which had been closed under Cromwell's Puritanical autocracy; in 1660, he was appointed along with Thomas Killigrew as one of the two theatrical patentees who obtained a monopoly of public theatre performances. In this capacity he headed the Duke of York's Men and produced highly successful theatrical seasons at Lincoln's Inn Fields from 1660 until his death eight years later. Among his more successful productions were some Shakespeare plays, including *King Lear*, *Hamlet*, *Henry VIII* and *The Tempest*. Davenant was about as far removed from the Puritanical spirit as it was possible to get. He was a committed *bon viveur* who in 1630 had contracted syphilis, for which he was treated by famous physician Thomas Cademan. This treatment, though saving Davenant's life, left him with a disfigured nose, which entertained his enemies and made him the butt of many jokes. The damage to Davenant's nose can be seen in the engraving made following John Greenhill's sympathetic portrait of him (available via the National Portrait Gallery online).

With Davenant's death came the end for well over 150 years of *King Lear* being performed as Shakespeare had written it. With the change in public tastes following the Restoration, the play was no longer popular in its original form.

Major changes in Tate's *King Lear*

In 1681 Nahum Tate (1652–1715), son of the gloriously named Irish Puritan clergyman Faithful Teate, rewrote *King Lear* to his own tastes. Tate – who had changed the family name on arriving in England – described Shakespeare's original as: 'a heap of jewels unstrung and unpolished'. Under Tate's confident zeal (''tis more difficult to save than 'tis to kill'), the play was enthusiastically re-constructed as a 'History':

◥ The Fool and the King of France disappear entirely.

◥ Cordelia does not leave for France, but stays in England and tries to find and save her father in the storm.

◥ Tate writes in a servant (Arante) in whom Cordelia can confide.

◥ Cordelia has an on-then-off-then-on-again love affair with Edgar.

◥ Edmund shows no last-minute kindness.

◥ Tate's Cordelia grants Edgar her love again only after he has saved her from being raped by a less psychologically complex Edmund, who has sent two thugs to abduct her and bring her to him.

◥ Cordelia and Edgar are united at the conclusion when the wicked receive their just desserts. (In Shakespeare's play, Edgar and Cordelia never speak to each other.)

Context

Tate's Puritan upbringing and Tory leanings were evident in his other re-workings of Shakespeare. He was so disconcerted that *Richard II* might give sustenance to Whigs, liberals and anti-monarchists that he re-wrote it as *The Sicilian Usurper* (1681), changing the characters' names, moving the action abroad, and altering the text so that every scene was 'full of respect to Majesty and the dignity of Courts.'

- Goneril and Regan secretly poison each other, instead of Goneril poisoning Regan and later stabbing herself.

- Gloucester – now renamed Gloster but still blind – survives the shock of learning the identity of Edgar.

- Lear, no longer frail but suddenly invigorated, kills not just one but two of the henchmen who attempt to hang Cordelia.

- In the nick of time Edgar and Albany arrive with a reprieve for Cordelia.

- Albany, who has just won the civil war in which the forces loyal to Lear were defeated, resigns the crown to the old king, and Lear instructs that 'Cordelia shall be Queen'.

- Lear gives Cordelia to Edgar in a betrothal: 'I wrong'd him too, but here's the fair amends', and the audience sees Edgar and Cordelia as future monarchs.

- Lear, Kent and Gloster retire 'to some cool cell', safe in the knowledge that Britain is about to be governed wisely and benevolently by Cordelia and Edgar, who happily exclaims at the conclusion: 'Truth and virtue shall at last succeed!'

Shakespeare's *King Lear* it is not, but the adaptation proved popular and Shakespeare's version was exiled to the theatrical equivalent of the wilderness.

Shakespeare's cosmic bleakness as revealed in *King Lear* did not appeal to Tate, who more than eighty years after the appearance of *The History of King Lear* was lauded for his endeavours by Samuel Johnson, who as we have seen (p.41) was so shaken by Cordelia's death that he could not bear to return to Shakespeare's original until paid to do so as an editor. Johnson loved what Tate had done with Cordelia: 'In the present case the public has decided. Cordelia from the time of Tate has always retired with victory and felicity.' Tate was not a figure of universal popularity, however, even in his own lifetime: his poems were savagely satirised by Alexander Pope in *The Dunciad* and Joseph Addison thought that Tate had 'mutilated' *King Lear*. But to no avail: Tate's version of the play, a 'History' cobbled together from a Tragedy with the ending of a Comedy, was uncommonly popular and unrivalled on stage. In fact, according to Sir Stanley Wells of the Shakespeare Institute, Tate's version was 'one of the longest-lasting successes of the English drama', completely supplanting Shakespeare 'in every performance given from 1681 to 1838.'

For all of its changes, Tate's version kept some of Shakespeare's original dialogue intact and is only some 800 lines shorter than the original. It was in *The History of King Lear* that David Garrick (1717–79) appeared in the title role several times between 1742 and 1776, winning praise for his presentation of the distressed, outcast father. Garrick was the instigator of a more naturalistic style of acting, replacing the deliberately grandiose 'bombastic' style popular from the seventeenth century. Garrick retained the whole of Tate for a famous 1742 production but did reintroduce a little more Shakespeare into the play in 1743 and again in 1756. At first Garrick presented his King Lear in modern dress

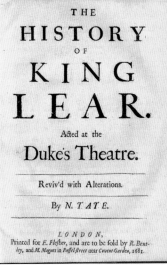

▲ Frontispiece of Nahum Tate's attempt to 'rectify what was wanting in the Regularity and Probability of the Tale'

but in later years he changed the setting to Ancient Britain, which became the established 'era' of the play until the more experimental and radical productions of the mid-twentieth century.

Garrick was described in performance as a 'little old white-haired man … with spindle shanks, a tottering gait and great shoes upon little feet…' (Sir John Hill, 1755) and was thus able to inculcate in the audience a sense that they were watching an ordinary man suffering and having to cope with extraordinary circumstances. It is reported that audiences were even able to cry in sympathy at Garrick's performance, though to modern tastes Lear's speech to Kent at the end – delivered in a jig of happy delirium – 'Why I have News that will recall thy Youth/Ha! Didst thou hear't, or did th' inspiring Gods/Whisper to me alone? Old Lear shall be/A King again' might precipitate tears of incredulous laughter in Shakespeare-lovers rather than catharsis.

In 1756 there was a so called Battle of the Actors, when Garrick's rival Spranger Barry mounted a rival production of the play and elected to use Tate's *The History of King Lear*. According to the poet and playwright Frances Brooke, who attended Barry's production, the whole house was moved to tears, though Brooke was nonplussed that both actors should both have given Tate's work 'the preference to Shakespeare's excellent original', and that Garrick, in particular, who was considered the superior talent, should 'prefer the adulterated cup of Tate to the pure genuine draught offered him by the master he avows to serve with such fervency of devotion'. Shakespeare aficionados had to rely on the printed version to get a flavour of the playwright's original intentions.

Since Davenant's theatrical heyday no actor had been given the opportunity to perform Lear's famous death scene as he expires over Cordelia's corpse. In 1823 Edmund Kean, encouraged by the essayists Charles Lamb and William Hazlitt, and utterly convinced of his own talent, restored the tragic ending but still left out the Fool and kept much of Tate for the early scenes. 'The London audience,' Kean told his wife, 'have no notion of what I can do till they see me over the dead body of Cordelia', but after some indifferent reviews even the uber-confident Kean reverted to Tate completely. The public really did seem to like to stick with Tate's version. It is non-threatening and conformist to an extreme degree.

In 1834 William Charles Macready (1793–1873) had the courage to restore the tragic ending; he had previously experienced Tate's version and had found it to be a 'miserable debilitation and disfigurement of Shakespeare's sublime tragedy'. He still excluded the Fool, however. In 1838, encouraged by the audience reaction to his partially restored *King Lear* of four years earlier, in which the audience 'broke out into loud applause in the fourth and fifth acts', Macready restored the Fool, casting attractive young actress Priscilla Horton in the role, and followed the pattern of Shakespeare's original, though much truncated and shortened. This production, following the vogue for an Ancient British setting, saw Macready surround his Lear with dolmens and huge druidic stone circles reminiscent of Stonehenge. It is to Macready that we need to turn for the first solid evidence that performing Lear was the actors' equivalent of performing the impossible. The part, clearly a daunting and difficult role to play, seems to have played on his mind. He wrote, 'In reflecting on Lear I begin to apprehend I cannot make an effective character of it. *I am oppressed with the magnitude of the thoughts he has to utter…*' (my italics). Macready was known for his scrupulous academic and cultural research before he played a role and it is to his credit that he saw the magnitude of Shakespeare's masterpiece, whereas Tate had seen something that needed to be 'rectified'.

Despite Macready's 1838 restoration – some would say salvation – of Shakespeare from the clutches of Nahum Tate, it was not until 1845 that Samuel Phelps (1804–78) restored the complete, original Shakespearean text. Phelps had worked under Macready at Drury Lane but as his opportunities were stifled he broke away to become one of the co-leasees at the Sadler's Wells Theatre, where he staged 34 Shakespeare plays between 1844 and 1862 and did a huge amount to restore Shakespeare's status as a writer of genius – who did not need to be re-written or improved. Though somewhat neglected today, Phelps as a director exerted a great educational impact on the public and on actors alike. He published an annotated edition of Shakespeare's plays in two volumes (1852–54), which also helped re-establish Shakespeare's greatness in the minds of the public and in a new generation of academics who cared for Shakespeare in performance. Thanks to Macready, and particularly Phelps, other than occasional 'curiosity performances' of *The History of King Lear* (such as the one staged by the Riverside Shakespeare Company in March 1985 at The Shakespeare Center in New York), the long and troublesome reign of Tate in the theatre was over.

The play in its full and dire tragic form arouses strong opinions even in modern times. In 1936 John Middleton Murry wrote about Shakespeare's 'uncontrollable despair'. This analysis was first expounded by Caroline Spurgeon (*Shakespeare's Imagery and What It Tells Us*, 1935), who sees the dominant image of the play as that of a human body in a variety of desperate and shocking poses: 'in anguished movement, tugged, wrenched, beaten, pierced, stung, scourged, dislocated, flayed, gashed, scalded, tortured and finally broken on the rack'. Frank Kermode (2000) finds the play to be Shakespeare's 'cruellest'.

Social context

There was a real-life scandal and court case that has an almost uncanny bearing on *King Lear*. There were upwards of fifty versions of the King Lear story available before Shakespeare's version, but in none of them does the old king go mad.

Brian Annesley, a wealthy Kentishman and elderly gentleman pensioner of Queen Elizabeth, had three daughters: Grace (married to Sir John Wildgoose), Christian (the wife of William, 3rd Baron Sandys), and the youngest, the unmarried Cordell. In 1603 Grace, with some encouragement from Christian, tried to have her father declared insane and incompetent on the grounds that Annesley was 'altogether unfit to govern himself or his estate'. It seems clear that the two eldest daughters

Build critical skills

Is it an unremarkable coincidence or very eerie that Annesley's loyal real-life third daughter, who did not come to the public's attention until 1603, was called Cordell and the loyal fictional third daughter of the 1595 play had been called Cordella? There are those who believe that there is something of the supernatural about *King Lear*.

Context

The Fool's witticism (II.4.236) that 'Winter's not gone yet, if the wild geese fly that way' can be taken as a reference to the behaviour of Grace Wildgoose and her husband in trying to take from her aged father what was legally his, on the grounds that he was mentally incompetent because of insanity.

wanted to be able to annex their father's property and take control. Cordell wrote to Robert Cecil, 1st Earl of Salisbury, however, to protest her older sisters' action on the grounds that her father's loyal service to the late queen deserved better 'than at his last gasp to be recorded and registered a lunatic'. Cordell urged Cecil to have her father's estate put under the care of Sir James Croft. Cecil agreed and Annesley made a will in favour of Cordell.

When Annesley died in July 1604 the Wildgooses contested the will, but the terms of the will favouring Cordell were upheld by the Court of Chancery. One of the executors of the will was a Sir William Harvey, third husband of the Dowager Countess of Southampton, the mother of Shakespeare's patron Henry Wriothesley, 3rd Earl of Southampton. (Harvey is also one of the many proposed candidates for the 'W.H.' of Shakespeare's sonnets.) The Dowager Countess died in 1607 and William Harvey married Cordell Annesley in July 1608. Thus Harvey was the stepfather of Shakespeare's patron and the playwright was in a position to have discovered this story not only from a public perspective (it was big news in 1603–04 and was kept before the public until 1608) but also from a private source.

It is a logical conclusion to draw that this real-life scandal helped not only to inspire the revival and publication of the old play *King Leir*, but also served as inspiration for Shakespeare to introduce the theme of Lear's madness into his version of the play.

Cultural context

Nature, the cosmos and humankind

The concept of the Great Chain of Being was developed in Ancient Greece by Plato (429–347 BCE) and Aristotle (384–322 BCE), whose ideas were taken up and synthesised by Plotinus in Rome around 260 BCE. Interestingly, Plotinus rejected as illogical the belief that the stars guide human fortune, arguing that such a belief led to moral turpitude as it gave people a ready-made excuse for their own bad behaviour. Plotinus, who believed the stars were 'ensouled' (given significance and meaning) by the 'One' (God), in turn influenced Augustine's theology, and from there inspired Thomas Aquinas (1225–74) and his followers.

Context

Aurelius Augustinus - 'St Augustine of Hippo', or just Augustine - (354-430) was a Christian Neo-Platonist who helped to merge the traditions of Greek philosophy and Judaeo-Christian religiosity. A towering figure of medieval philosophy, Augustine believed that we must be morally responsible for our willed actions but that grace can save our souls. Again, *King Lear* is a frightening play because Cordelia - full of grace in Augustinian terms - dies with no promise of heavenly reward: 'Is this the promised end?'

The Great Chain of Being was an important theme in Renaissance thought. It started as a static world view but began gradually to include the concept of the soul ascending through successive spheres, thus growing or evolving closer to God. The early alchemists, such as Queen Elizabeth's mathematics tutor Doctor John Dee, believed that which is 'base' in creation could be impelled to aspire higher by refinement. Hence a base metal like lead could be worked on (refined) to make it 'nobler', like gold. The belief that there could be movement within the Chain slowly gained ground but was considered by many to be a suspect belief coming close to heresy – theories that expressed discontent at God's natural order were viewed by social and religious conservatives as worrying.

It is important to understand the internal tensions created within this dynamic. The Great Chain of Being is static and yet not quite static; comforting in that everything in nature has an allotted place, but troubling because aspiration enabled some movement. Puritans, the religious fundamentalists of their day, were caught in an intellectual and moral quandary by it: they were themselves rebellious, wanting to purify (refine) an impure religion (Catholicism), but were deeply worried by the thought of too much change. The Renaissance unleashed tensions that made people feel both excited and frightened. 'Truths' that had been reliable and comforting for hundreds of years were being questioned, and for every person who welcomed the New Learning of the Renaissance, there were others who felt threatened by it. It is particularly useful to see Shakespeare's plays as the dramatic manifestation of these tensions – between old, comfortable, conservative belief systems and new, challenging, liberating discoveries.

It is also important to consider that Shakespeare is perhaps more interested in making his audience react philosophically (and of course emotionally) to the questions he poses than he is in answering those questions.

Raymond de Sebonde (d. 1426) considered the Chain and recorded his thoughts in *Natural Theology*, a work that was translated from Latin into French in 1569 by Montaigne (whose name keeps cropping up in relation to *King Lear*):

> First there is mere existence, the inanimate class: the elements, liquids, and metals. But in spite of this common lack of life there is vast difference of virtue; water is nobler than earth, the ruby than the topaz, gold than brass: the links in the chain are there. Next there is existence and life, the vegetative class, where again the oak is nobler than the bramble. Next there is existence life and feeling, the sensitive class. In it there are three grades. First are the creatures having touch but not hearing, memory or movement. Such are shellfish and parasites on the base of trees. Then there are animals having touch, memory and movement but not hearing, for instance ants. And finally there are the higher animals, horse and dogs and their like, that have all these faculties. The three classes lead up to man, who has not only existence, life and feeling, but understanding: he sums up in himself the total faculties of earthly phenomena.

TASK

How far do you agree with the view that if we approach *King Lear* as a play that presents philosophical debates in highly symbolic ways, we will find more to enjoy in it and learn from it than if we approach it from the grounds of whether the characters are believable or their behaviour consistent with notions of social realism?

These ideas were still more or less in vogue up to the early seventeenth century.

The Chain of Being, like the Wheel of Fortune, presented a visual image of a complex idea about an interlocking universe where no part was superfluous; it celebrated and explained the dignity of all creation, even the meanest part of it.

Context

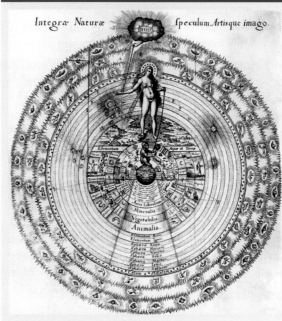

▲ Robert Fludd's conception of the world, 1617

Robert Fludd in this illustration depicts the correspondence between the human (the Ape of Nature) and the universe, as the human is held by a Great Chain of Being from the hand of God (inside cloud). Higher beings descended from God's heaven through the starry sphere and planetary orbits to the sphere of the four elements. Humans were thought to contain essences of all other parts of the universe. Fludd believed that sublimations and transformations were possible within alchemy and for humans.

The apparently superfluous could be put low down on the ladder of creation and effectively ignored. Shakespeare seems to question the traditional view of superfluity in *King Lear*, however, when Lear, who has been a traditionalist, moves into an ultra-modern and controversial view: the superfluous is not 'lowly' but essential. Via a redistribution of that which is left over, Lear understands that he will be able to help the poor.

Edmund is caustic in his rejection of the conventional view (that the stars following God's instruction are responsible for the fortunes of mankind), as this enables people to blame their bad behaviour on the influence of the stars rather than as being due to free will. He agrees with Plotinus but argues the case with sinister relish, illustrating his own will to power:

This is the excellent foppery of the world, that when we are sick in fortune, often the surfeits of our own behaviour, we make guilty of our disasters the sun, the moon and the stars, as if we were villains on necessity, fools by heavenly compulsion, knaves, thieves and treachers by spherical predominance; drunkards, liars and adulterers by an enforced obedience of planetary influence … Fut! I should have been that I am had the maidenliest star in the firmament twinkled on my bastardizing.

(I.2.118–33)

One of the reasons an audience can like Edmund, wicked though he is, is that he shapes his own destiny, believes in free will and makes no foppish or superstitious excuses for his behaviour. In this way he is a modern sort of character in a play that contains some very medieval characters.

Charles de Bovelles

A fascinating pictorial diagram from a work never translated into English is reproduced below. The pictogram is by Charles de Bovelles and first appeared around 1511.

Context

The Church occupied a difficult theological space: when Christianity was young there was wide belief in astrology. The Church tried to reduce the superstition associated with astrology but also wanted to assert that the stars moved in accordance with God's will and since such things as the pull of the moon on tides and planetary movement were self-evident truths, churchmen reasoned that astrology was part of the divine plan.

◀ Charles de Bovelles' 'Pyramid of the Living'

Charles de Bovelles ('Bovillus' in Latin, 1475–1566) was a French mathematician whose *Géométrie en Françoys* (1511) was the first scientific work to be printed in French. He wrote a Renaissance masterpiece still little known in the English-speaking world, entitled *Liber de Sapiente* (*The Book of Wisdom*), which was translated from its original Latin once into Italian and twice into French.

Key: **Latin**	English
MINERALE PETRA EST	MINERAL ROCK EXISTS
VEGETABILE ARBOR VIVIT EST	VEGETABLE TREE LIVES EXISTS
SENSIBILE EQUUS SENTIT VIVIT EST	SENSATE HORSE FEELS LIVES EXISTS
RATIONALE HOMO INTELLIGIT SENTIT VIVIT EST	RATIONAL MAN THINKS FEELS LIVES EXISTS
VIRTUS STUDIOSIS INTELLIGIT SENTIT VIVIT EST	VIRTUE SCHOLARLY THINKS FEELS LIVES EXISTS
LUXURIA SENSUALIS SENTIT VIVIT EST	LUST SENSUAL FEELS LIVES EXISTS
GULA VITALIS VIVIT EST	GLUTTONS LIVE EXIST
ACEDIA MINERALIS EST	SLOTH INSENSATE EXISTS

Context

Ernst Cassirer (1874-1945) was a major figure in the development of twentieth-century philosophical idealism. A German Jew, he fled the Nazis in 1933. Cassirer developed a philosophy of culture as a theory of symbols founded in what he termed a phenomenology of knowledge. Man, says Cassirer in his 'Essay on Man' (1944), is a 'symbolic animal'.

In *The Individual and the Cosmos in Renaissance Philosophy* (1927), the twentieth-century philosopher Ernst Cassirer wrote that *Liber de Sapiente* is 'perhaps the most curious and in some respects the most characteristic creation of Renaissance philosophy … because in no other work can we find such an intimate union of old and new ideas'. Unlike the ideal of the wise as made wise by God, found in the late medieval wisdom literature, Bovelles' wise man creates his own identity. In *Liber de Sapiente*, the wise man has developed his own sense of wisdom through two stages of knowledge: the first stage was of things in the 'sublunar world' through the senses; the second stage was the soul's own contemplation of itself, which Bovelles was probably aware of via Socrates: 'O Homo, nosce te ipsum' ('O Man, know thyself (and thou will know the universe and the gods)'.)

Whereas animal behaviour is instinctive and motivated by sensory perception, Bovelles argued that man's behaviour is motivated by more complex triggers. For Bovelles, humans gave symbolic significance to important things in their life and were able to consider such issues as human improvement in relation to ideas about shared human culture. Cassirer believed that symbolic forms of thought and expression (linguistic, scholarly, scientific and artistic) allowed humans to improve and refine themselves, which eventually led to a kind of self-discovery and liberation. Cassirer believed that Bovelles had been the originator of most of these important ideas.

Edmund can be interpreted as a character initially trapped by circumstances beyond his control, condemned by his illegitimacy to live on the outskirts of society. He knows that his attributes and individual resources (his 'dimensions') are not inferior to those of his 'legitimate' brother and so embarks on a quest of self-realisation and self-actualisation, powered by the force of his own free will. There can be something darkly admirable and modern about his quest. Though also powered by free will, Goneril's and Regan's rebellion against their father is not, unlike Edmund's, motivated by an authentic desire for self-realisation and fulfilment but instead is merely a selfish quest for status and power. In this sense they can be seen as irrevocably medieval. According to Bovelles, once self-knowledge is attained the soul may progress to the contemplation of simpler and purer perfection, most usually associated in Renaissance thought with angels, and finally to participate in the sublime wisdom of God – the source of all true wisdom.

Evidently neither Edmund nor the wicked sisters wishes to use their self-knowledge as a starting point for the contemplation of perfection, but Edgar does become what Bovelles calls a 'thrice-man'. The wise man is 'thrice-man':

1   Man by nature – by having a human body and soul.

2   Man by human physical development – by age.

3   Man by fully developing the potential of his own spirit, which according to Bovelles will be virtuous but, in reality, of course, may not be so.

Albany undoubtedly becomes wiser as the play develops and, unlike the wicked Edmund, does develop his own virtuous spirit once he learns to liberate himself from the dominant influence of Goneril. Arguably, both Lear and Gloucester also become 'thrice-men'. Because Bovelles argues that humanity can be developed through personal effort of will, he endorses not the medieval conception of man being made wise by the grace of God but instead by the force of man's own abilities to act independently, of his own free will. In this sense man can operate independently, outside the imagined forces of the Great Chain of Being. Bovelles explores some startling ideas reminiscent of modern semiology: in human affairs, pictures, images and objects (e.g. flags, football colours and logos) that carry symbolic importance are profoundly important for the individual.

In many ways Bovelles' *Liber de Sapiente* can be described as the first description of what is now termed human psychology: humans ascribe importance to signs because they carry symbolic value for them as individuals, and not necessarily because the signs are the manifestations of a divine will. Bovelles, then, understood the importance of symbols and laid the ground for modern semiology. Critics, readers and audiences (such as Tolstoy) who do not enjoy *King Lear* do not interpret the play symbolically but criticise it because, for example, it is not true to the values of social realism.

Could Shakespeare have read Bovelles? Yes, if he visited the Catholic Colleges in Rome or Douai (see p.71 above), where Bovelles was read and admired. A Latin or French copy could easily have found its way into England.

A careful reading of *King Lear* reveals much of Bovelles' thought. For example, there is a tantalising verbal echo of Bovelles in III.6.22, when Lear in his madness calls the Fool 'sapient sir'. In his pictorial diagram (see p.71) Bovelles drew the human equivalent of *Petra* literally as a Man of Stone. When Lear carries Cordelia in his arms in Act V he rails at the assembled characters 'O, you are men of stones!' (line 255) because they cannot feel the depth of his own enormous loss. Bovelles draws a vain, mirror-gazing, effeminate fop to represent *Luxuria*; in Kent's diatribe against Oswald in Act II scene 2 he calls him (among other insults)

CRITICAL VIEW

Frank Kermode (1975), distrustful of criticism that seeks to redefine the play for each successive generation of academics, claims 'King Lear subsists in change, by being patient of interpretation.' Thus Kermode makes the case that the play's importance is timeless and there is something about the way it addresses the human condition that will keep it always relevant, whatever critical views are fashionable at any given time.

CRITICAL VIEW

Roy W. Battenhouse (in 'Moral experience and its typology in King Lear', 1965, reprinted in Shakespearean Tragedy, 1969) offers a Christian analysis of the play, viewing Cordelia as initially selfish. Her later experiences of love, however, inspire her to cast off her former preoccupation with the self.

a 'shallow', 'lily-livered', 'glass-gazing', 'super-serviceable', 'finical', 'neat', 'cullionly barber-monger', 'rogue', 'bawd', 'pander' and 'varlet' – perhaps the most comprehensive description of *Luxuria Sensualis* found on the English stage. In his madness in Act IV scene 6, Lear cries 'To't, luxury, pell-mell' (line 115). When Edgar in the guise of Poor Tom tells Lear in Act III scene 4 what has brought him to this sorry plight, he traces his fall through Bovelles' stages of decline, from *Luxuria* ('A serving-man … that curled my hair … served the lust of my mistress' heart' and 'slept in the contriving of lust'), to *Gula* ('Wine loved I deeply, dice dearly'), to the final stage of *Acedia* (a 'hog in sloth', lines 83–91).

Critical context

To an interested, open-minded student, reading the opinions of others is always enjoyable: we can see things that we have not ourselves considered, and are able to see the play much more 'in-the-round'. Many references to critics useful to you in your examination have been integrated throughout this guide. It is fair to say that since *King Lear* is a drama, the most useful critical opinions will be aware of the play on stage and will analyse the language the playwright creates for the characters. Students, however, must exercise judgement and discrimination. A good general rule at A-level is that when the critical analysis begins with the play (language, stage directions, dramatic potentials) and moves out from the text to its contexts, the criticism will be valid and useful. Some critics, however, have their own pet theory or world view. They then try to find evidence for this theory in the literature that they read. This is putting the context before the text and can be a most unhelpful model for A-level. Be prepared to disagree or argue with some of the viewpoints you read. Not all criticism is necessarily illuminating or worth agreeing with.

Important concerns for modern critics have involved gender roles, ideas about patriarchy and its influence on the family and state, the position of women, and the relation of *King Lear* to social and economic forces of Shakespeare's time. Ideas about religion and philosophy are still very important.

Read the critical observations on these pages. Some of the ideas are text-led whereas others are context-led. If you find an interesting idea that you want to research further, explore the critic on the internet or in a good library: be sure to make notes of where you encounter the articles you read so you can build up a critical bibliography. Decide which of the analyses of *King Lear* encourage you to want to explore the criticism more fully.

◥ Lawrence Rosinger (in 'Gloucester and Lear: Men who Act like Gods', 1968) claims the play is about Gloucester's and Lear's self-discovery after a period of treating others as a means of self-gratification. This analysis which blends Aristotelian Classicism with a touch of Freud makes the play very male-centric and argues that hubris develops in correlation to the characters' ages.

◥ Rosalie L. Colie (in *Some Facets of 'King Lear'*, 1974) claims the play is a commentary on fathers losing their power in a particular and measurable historical period. This view which explores the paradoxical nature of the biblical echoes in *King Lear* places the play at a particular time in history and therefore devalues the notion that the play is for all time. *Some Facets of King Lear* is a collection of twelve essays from what Cole, who was the project's editor, termed the 'Prismatic' school of Criticism. Cole attempts to present the twelve essays as though they are 'facets of a prism', all unique but 'mutually supportive'.

◣ Stephen Greenblatt (ed.) (in *The Power of Forms in the English Renaissance*, 1982), contends that Lear 'wishes to be the object – the preferred and even the sole recipient – of his child's love'. The play's central concern, therefore, is Lear's selfishness. Greenblatt is regarded as one of the founders of New Historicism.

◣ Investigating the overlap between familial and state politics in the world of the play, Kathleen McLuskie in 'The patriarchal bard: feminist criticism and *King Lear*' (1985) explores the relationship between power and gender, finding that 'insubordination' by female characters results in chaos, as it threatens the balance of power within the family: women with opinions frighten men. This traditional feminist analysis sees the play as a male retreat from emerging female power leading to a world of chaos.

◣ Peter Erickson (in *Patriarchal Structures in Shakespeare's Drama*, 1985) thinks the play is essentially about male bonding, arguing that although Lear tries to counter the loss of his daughters with the fellowship of his 'knights', these male bonds are 'finally a minor resource compared with the unequivocal centrality of Cordelia for Lear': this view infers that though male bonding is desired by men it is clearly not as important as love within the family. Erickson's criticism is an extension of feminism whose importance Erickson acknowledges though he argues that the work of such feminist critics as Marilyn French in *Shakespeare's Division of Experience* (1983), that sees patriarchy as fixed, is 'reductive'. Erickson argues that patriarchy is 'not monolithic but multivalent'.

◣ Marxist critic Terry Eagleton (*Sweet Violence: The Idea of the Tragic*, 2008) thinks that the tragic theories attached to most criticism of *King Lear* have been 'pious waffle': watching Lear's affliction makes the audience desire political liberation. Eagleton sees the play as a proto-Marxist tract, making the audience dissatisfied with the way society is constructed and seeking social change.

◣ Germaine Greer (the *Guardian*, 2008) calls *King Lear* 'the greatest metaphysical poem in the English language' and believes the importance of the play lies in its symbolism and use of language. Though a feminist, Greer thinks the play's importance goes beyond issues of gender and politics.

Directors' contexts

Kath Bradley of the Royal Shakespeare Company and The Shakespeare Institute, University of Birmingham, has conducted research into which are the key scenes in the play by canvassing the opinions of directors of *King Lear*. Bradley arranged a chronological sequence of the ten most important scenes, in terms of what directors of *King Lear* had nominated as scenes of vital importance. Careful A-level students demonstrate via their work that knowledge of the *theatrical* potentials of the play is of paramount importance in demonstrating good understanding of the genre, and such students work hard to analyse and explore the dramatic as well as the thematic and literary importance of the following 'key' scenes:

1 **Lear divides the kingdom** (Act 1 scene 3)
   Lear announces his intention to split his kingdom into three and asks which of his daughters loves him most. He banishes Cordelia for not pandering to him, and splits his land between Regan and Goneril, who lie.

2 **Edmund lies to Gloucester** (Act 1 scene 2)
   In a parallel development to how Lear is deceived by his daughters Goneril and Regan, Gloucester is deceived by his son Edmund, whose Machiavellian genius forces Gloucester to doubt the loyalty of his other son, Edgar.

3 **Lear is cast out into the storm** (Act 2 scene 2)
   Enraged by his daughters' refusal to allow him to keep his one hundred knights, the vulnerable and 'unaccommodated' Lear and his Fool walk out into the eye of the storm, as Cornwall bars the gates of Gloucester's castle behind them.

4 **'Poor Tom'** (Act 3 scene 4)
   Lear, Kent and the Fool meet Edgar, disguised as Poor Tom, on the heath and are persuaded to take refuge in a hovel as the counterfeit lunatic babbles his way through Harsnett's litany of devils (see p.61).

5 **Gloucester is blinded** (Act 3 scene 5)
   Gloucester is accused by Goneril and Regan of treachery to the new regime for sending Lear to meet Cordelia's army. His eyes are savagely plucked out and he is thrown out of his own castle so he can 'smell his way to Dover'. Cornwall is killed by one of his own servants.

6 **Cordelia searches for her father** (Act 4 scene 3)
   As they prepare for imminent battle against the forces of darkness represented by her sisters, Cordelia and her army hear news of the mad king and, in an attempt to offer love and forgiveness, set out to find him.

7 **Gloucester and Lear are rescued** (Act 4 scene 5)
   Gloucester, led by 'Poor Tom', is saved from suicide by his son's trickery. They then meet Lear and are reconciled. Lear is found and helped by Cordelia's troops.

8 **Lear and Cordelia are reunited** (Act 4 scene 6)
   The king recovers his wits and is reconciled with Cordelia.

9 **Edmund's plot** (Act 5 scene 7)
   Edmund reveals that he has seduced both sisters and that he intends to kill both Lear and Cordelia if his side wins the battle.

10 **The tragic ending** (Act 5 scene 3)
   Cordelia's French army loses the battle, after which both she and her father are imprisoned. Edmund's plot is exposed and he is killed by Edgar in a duel. Goneril stabs herself after poisoning Regan. Cordelia is hanged on Edmund's instructions. Lear dies of grief when he learns that both Gloucester and the Fool are also dead.

Assessment Objectives and skills

The five key English Literature Assessment Objectives (AOs) describe the different skills you need to show in order to get a good grade. Regardless of what texts or which examination specification you are following, the AOs lie at the heart of your study of English literature; they let you know exactly what the examiners are looking for and provide a helpful framework for your literary studies.

The Assessment Objectives require you to:

AO1 **Articulate informed, personal and creative responses to literary texts, using associated concepts and terminology, and coherent, accurate written expression.**

- ◄ AO1 requires informed and accurately written relevant responses that make effective use of appropriate concepts and terminology.

- ◄ It also expects that students will have reached their own reasoned critique about literary texts.

- ◄ In some ways this idea links to AO5; it may be helpful to think of the AOs not as a list but as a circle of requirements, so that the end of AO5 'feeds into' the beginning of AO1.

AO2 **Analyse ways in which meanings are shaped in literary texts.**

- ◄ AO2 requires students to analyse ways in which meanings are shaped in literary texts, with particular focus on the structures of texts as a form of shaping. Interesting ideas about structure will relate to language.

- ◄ For example, part of Shakespeare's structure will link to his decisions about language. Lear's fury in the early part of the play is conveyed in his references to himself as the embodiment of a vengeful dragon, and his bitterness against his daughters is conveyed via his highly anatomical curses and insults, many of which feature animal imagery. By Act 3 his language has become more judicial and is also frequently shot through with references to religion, in particular guilt, sin and prayer. By Act 4 his mad mind teems with images of money, militarism, marital infidelity and copulation, though he is still obsessed with preaching about hell and darkness. By Act 5 the stark religious imagery is replaced by an altogether more benign sort of religious language, featuring benediction, grace and forgiveness.

- ◄ The most successful students will thus link structure and language within AO2.

> **AO3 Demonstrate understanding of the significance and influence of the contexts in which literary texts are written and received.**
>
> ▼ AO3 relates to the many possible contexts that arise out of the text, the specific task and the period being studied.
>
> **AO4 Explore connections across literary texts.**
>
> ▼ AO4 involves connections across texts. It sees possible meanings and interpretations arising not only out of the contexts of the text itself (AO3) but also out of the wider and broader contexts that come from the study of the era. Thus, even when an individual text is being investigated, it should still be seen as being framed by a wider network of texts and contexts to which it connects.
>
> **AO5 Explore literary texts informed by different interpretations.**
>
> ▼ AO5 completes the picture by acknowledging that if work in AOs 2, 3 and 4 have been included in the response to the question then debate and interpretations will arise out of this work, showing that the interpretation of texts is not a fixed process but a dynamic one.

Examination questions are written with the AOs in mind, so if you answer the questions clearly and carefully while thinking about the AOs, you should hit the right targets. If you are devising your own questions for coursework, seek the help of your teacher to ensure that your essay title is carefully worded to liberate the required Assessment Objectives so that you can do your best.

Although the Assessment Objectives are common to all the exam boards, each specification varies in the way it meets the requirements. For example, if you are studying AQA Specification A you will need to give special attention to the concept of historicity, which the board explain thus:

> *English Literature A's historicist approach to the study of literature rests upon reading texts within a shared context. Working from the belief that no text exists in isolation but is the product of the time in which it was produced, English Literature A encourages students to explore the relationships that exist between texts and the contexts within which they are written, received and understood. Studying texts within a shared context enables students to investigate and connect them, drawing out patterns of similarity and difference using a variety of reading strategies and perspectives.*

The boards' websites provide useful information, including sections for students, past papers, sample papers and mark schemes. You are advised to make use of them.

- ▼ AQA: www.aqa.org.uk
- ▼ Edexcel: www.edexcel.com
- ▼ OCR: www.ocr.org.uk
- ▼ WJEC: www.wjec.co.uk

Remember, though, that your knowledge and understanding of the text still lies at the heart of A-level study, as it always has done. In the end, the study of literature starts with, and comes back to, your own engagement with the text itself.

Building skills 1: Structuring your writing

This section focuses on organising your written responses to convey your ideas as clearly and effectively as possible: the 'how' of your writing as opposed to the 'what'. More often than not, if your knowledge and understanding of *King Lear* is sound, a disappointing mark or grade will be down to one of two common mistakes: misreading the question, or failing to organise your response economically and effectively. In an examination you'll be lucky if you can demonstrate 5 per cent of what you know about *King Lear*; luckily, if it's the right 5 per cent, that's all you need to gain full marks.

Understanding your examination

It's important to prepare for the specific type of response your examination body sets with regard to *King Lear*. You'll almost certainly know whether you are studying the play as part of a non-examined assessment unit (i.e. for coursework) or as an examination set text – but you also need to know if your paper is open book (in which case, you will have a clean copy of the text available to you in the exam) or closed book (in which case, you won't). The format of your assessment has major implications for the way you organise your response and dictates the depth and detail required to achieve a top band mark.

Open book

In an open book exam, where you have a copy of *King Lear* on the desk in front of you, there can be no possible excuse for failing to quote relevantly, accurately and extensively. To gain a high mark, you are expected to focus in detail on specific passages. Remember, too, that you must not refer to any supporting material such as the Introductory Notes contained within the set edition of your text. If an examiner suspects that you have been lifting chunks of unacknowledged material from such a source, they will refer your paper to the examining body for possible plagiarism.

Closed book

In a closed book exam, because the examiner is well aware that you do not have the text in front of you, their expectations will be different. While you are still expected to support your argument with relevant quotations, close textual references are also rewarded. Since you will have had to memorise quotations, slight inaccuracies will not be severely punished.

Non-examined assessment (NEA)

Writing about *King Lear* within a non-examined assessment (coursework) context poses a very different set of challenges from an examination, in that incorrect quotations and disorientating arguments are liable to cost you much more dearly. Your essay must be wholly and consistently relevant to the title selected; there's no excuse for going off-track if you or your teacher have mapped out the parameters of your chosen topic in the first place. Wider reading is very important at A-level and you may need to compare and contrast *King Lear* to other texts you have studied. Be careful to check the appropriate weightings for the relevant Assessment Objectives outlined by your particular exam board. As well as ensuring your title clearly addresses the relevant AOs and allows for adequate, focused treatment within the set word limit, there are a number of crucial stages in the writing process for non-examined assessment:

- Discuss your proposed title with your teacher as soon as possible.
- Plan your essay. Have tutorials with your teacher and make use of their advice.
- Identify any background reading, such as textual criticism, that may be useful to you, gather the articles and books you need, read them and make notes.
- Give yourself sufficient time to draft the work, analysing your text, making notes, and keeping and filing other useful materials.
- Keep referring back to the title or question to make sure you remain focused on it.
- Allow time for your teacher to read and comment on your draft.
- Redraft and proofread your essay before handing it in, and ensure that you have maintained your focus on the relevant AOs.
- A bibliography should list all the texts you have consulted and will demonstrate your learning and referencing. Check with your teacher whether you are required to use any particular format for a bibliography and if so stick to this.

Locate the debate

A very common type of exam question invites you to open up a debate about the text by using various trigger words and phrases, such as **'Consider the view that...'**, **'Some critics think that...'** or **'How far do you agree that...?'** When analysing this type of question, the one thing you can be sure of is that exam questions never offer a view that makes no sense at all or one so blindingly obvious that all anyone can do is agree with it; there will always be a genuine interpretation at stake. Similarly, many NEA tasks are written to include a stated view to help give some shape to your writing, so logically your introduction needs to orientate the reader by addressing the terms of this debate and sketching out the outline of how you intend to move the argument forward.

Since it's obviously going to be helpful if you actually know this before you start writing, you really do need to plan before you begin to write.

Undertaking a lively debate about some of the ways in which *King Lear* has been and can be interpreted is the DNA of your essay. Of course, any good argument needs to be honest; but to begin by writing 'Yes, I totally agree with this obviously true statement' suggests a fundamental misunderstanding of what studying literature is all about. The stated views in examination questions are designed to open up critical conversations, not to shut them down.

Plan your answer by collecting together points for and against the given view. Aim to see a stated opinion as an interesting way of focusing upon a key facet of *King Lear*.

Student A

Here is an example of the sort of question that will be asked on the WJEC specification:

'Shakespeare's presentation of the Fool merely contributes to the addition of comic relief within *King Lear*.' Examine this view of the play.

There's a world of difference between a Clown and a Fool. Shakespeare's principal comedian had been Will Kemp, who specialised in low humour and physical comedy. Praised as the finest clown of his generation, Kemp specialised in rural simpletons and was the kind of ad-libbing performer prone to dancing jigs and singing extempore. Kemp enjoyed solo improvisation, puns, direct bawdry, physical contortions and mangling language. He was hugely popular and it was said that he did a visual gag with a custard pie and a pint of beer that left the audience in gales of laughter. Sadly no record of what the gag entailed survives. However, what we can assume with some degree of certainty is that Kemp's clowning was either mere low comedy or comic relief in the more serious moments of the early Tragedies and Histories.

In 1599 Kemp sold his share in The Lord Chamberlain's Men and jigged off to Norwich. With Kemp's departure Shakespeare's Company encountered the congenial Robert Armin. Muriel Bradbrook in Shakespeare the Craftsman defines the sort of qualities Armin brought to the role: the Fool now attended ladies (though Lear's fool significantly does not do so, being seemingly afraid of Goneril and not appearing on stage with Cordelia, leaving the potential for doubling-up of those parts), was presented in contrast with rogues and villains, lived outside the social order, is bitter and deflationary, and is given to music and song. Lear's Fool fits most of these criteria. With Armin's arrival Shakespeare created the parts of professional fools as wise men under camouflage. Armin was not only an actor but a writer: his book *Foole upon Foole* and his pamphlets were well received. Under the pseudonym of Clunnico del Vurtanio Snuffle, Armin wrote about the world as a subject of folly and held a view of folly similar to Erasmus, who coined the term 'foolosopher'. To have a 'witty fool' such as Armin on the books makes it extremely unlikely that the playwright would want to use his talents for mere comic relief.

G.L. Evans ('Shakespeare's fools', 1972) puts forward the view that the Fool is 'the repository of the most important truths *King Lear* has to communicate'. Under Armin's stewardship, the Fool began to develop a psychological relationship with the Jacobean audience and began to represent their views and feelings, the Fool's remarks being those that the audience would wish to make if they were clever enough or close enough to the action. Armin was 'a cultural commentator on the new uncertainties of Stuart England, to which the whole company had now to be responsive.' (P. Thomson, *Shakespeare's Professional Career* 1992). If we agree with Thomson there is far more than providing comic relief which the part of the Fool brings to 'King Lear'.

Lear's Fool is not named as Kemp was rather obviously as Costard (but no beer) for example in *Love's Labour's Lost* and has no identity except for the recognition of his status and job-description as Lear's fool. The King and his wise Fool are inextricably linked; the Fool is Lear's other self, debating with him and revealing to him his predicament whereby the King eventually knows himself as a fool, as all of his other titles he has 'given away'. He holds a special licence, the right to speak his mind which he exercises in order to make the King see his own folly. Despite his comparatively minor role in terms of the number of lines he is given and his early death, the role of the fool is central to the progress of the play in terms of its moral direction: no provider of low comic relief, he. The honest man caught up in the growing cruelty and depravity of Goneril's, Regan's and Edmund's New Order, the Fool delivers caustic sermons:

'I had rather be any kind o' thing than a fool: and yet I would not be thee Nuncle; thou hast pared thy wit o' both sides, and left nothing i' the middle' (I.iv.181–184)

The fool becomes Lear's teacher or confessor guiding him to a crucial knowledge of the truth and giving him a vision of the real world: 'Thou wast a pretty fellow when thou hadst no need to care for her frowning; now thou art an O without a figure. I am better than thou art now; I am a Fool, thou art nothing.' (I.iv.188–191)

During Cordelia's long absence from the stage between acts I and IV it could be argued that the Fool acts as a cipher for her, never letting Lear or the audience forget her. It is perhaps for this reason, more than any other that many directors double-up the roles. His anger and bewilderment at Lear's treatment of his youngest daughter expresses itself in savage attacks – in snatches of ballads, in doggerel poetry and in excoriating sarcasm. He calls Lear a 'fool' on twelve different occasions. Tolstoy argued that the Fool's jokes are not 'witty' but he may have a point. The Fool in 'telling the same joke a dozen times' (Adrian Scarborough who played him at the National in 2014) is metaphorically hitting Lear over the head with reminders of his own stupidity. However the Fool moves beyond mere comedy and comic relief and hence Tolstoy surely misses the subtlety of the Fool and the importance of his role. Shakespeare is writing for (and possibly with) Armin, not Kemp, so our playwright gives the Fool the job of reintroducing the leitmotif of 'nothing', claiming that nothing is what his 'Nuncle' (mine uncle) has become. There is a smack of Henry VIII's fool Will Sommers in the affectionate use of the word 'nuncle'. Henry reformed the Church which was a grievous and bizarre act to many people and similarly Lear has inverted the natural order by giving away his kingdom so the Fool also reminds Lear of his crimes against Nature: 'thou mad'st thy daughters thy mothers' (I, iv lines 163–64).When Lear asks: 'Who is it that can tell me who I am?' (I, iv line 227), the Fool's answer 'Lear's shadow' underlines how Lear losing his status and former dignity has reduced him to a ghost within his own lifetime. The Fool's comedy is the polar opposite of comic relief: it is searchingly thought-provoking, philosophical and troubling for the audience. By the time the Fool disappears bearing off his friend the King after his last words that he will go to bed at noon in Act III Lear has fallen and the Fool has provided a running commentary of that awful descent. 'The King having lost everything, including his wits, has now himself become the fool. He has touched bottom, he is an outcast from society, he has no longer any private axe to grind, so now he sees and speaks the truth.' (Frank Kermode, Shakespeare's 'King Lear') Once the King has been stripped of all his assets, and of his lies, he is forced to see the truth and it is the Fool who represents this voice after Cordelia's departure into exile. The Fool does not provide comic relief in 'King Lear': His dark comedy illuminates the nihilistic darkness.

Examiner's commentary

- ❧ The response is sophisticated, perceptive and analytical in all AOs.
- ❧ The candidate successfully understands that the word 'merely' is a key differentiator in the question and keeps the idea of the Fool merely providing comic relief at the heart of a very well-informed and extremely interesting answer.
- ❧ The early focus on Kemp is excellent because the candidate makes great use of her splendid knowledge: Kemp was a gifted clown and his performances in earlier plays such as *Love's Labour's Lost* may well have been for mere comic relief.
- ❧ The candidate makes splendid use of historicity: when Armin replaced Kemp in 1599 it gave Shakespeare the opportunity to refine the function of the theatrical clown and make it more of a 'wise man under camouflage'. The candidate traces the word 'Nuncle' to Henry VIII's licensed fool, Will Sommers.
- ❧ Critics Bradbrook, Evans, Thomson and Kermode are all used to support the candidate's argument, as are the views of modern-day actor Adrian Scarborough. The candidate has the confidence to disagree with Tolstoy.
- ❧ The argument is clear and compelling throughout: Lear's Fool provides far more than comic relief; he gives caustic sermons, is Lear's guide and confessor, and his dark comedy illuminates the play.

Written under exam conditions with a few related AO1 SPaG issues – no doubt due to examination pressures – this represents the very best sort of A-level work and the candidate would receive a mark of the very highest order. There is no reason not to award this essay an A*.

Student B

Here is an example of the sort of question that will be asked on the Edexcel specification:

Explore Shakespeare's presentation of Goneril and Regan in *King Lear*. You must relate your discussion to relevant contextual factors and ideas from your critical reading.

In 'King Lear' Goneril and Regan reach the point where, after being allied to each other, they fight each other for power. Shakespeare presents Goneril and Regan as aggressive, forceful and destructive. They are capable of almost anything as they appear to have no conscience when dealing with their father or each other. The Elizabethan status quo was based on notions of loyalty and bonds, especially within monarchies and inside the family unit. Under the new order in the play, bonds are broken and loyalty is replaced by greed and lust for power. Cordelia gives a modern audience some implication of the power and affection of a bond when the greatest expression of love she can give to her father is: 'I love your majesty / According to my bond, no more nor less.' Although in the modern day this may seem formal and a bit frigid (especially in contrast to her sisters exaggerated claims of love), for the era it was a kind of ultimate truth, a sort of perfection which went as far as necessary without going too far. Shakespeare's 'King Lear', is a tragedy written between 1603 and 1606. Goneril and Regan will do anything to get what they want. They are completely power-mad and malicious, turn to violence easily and are not troubled by any sense of remorse for anything they do. Some critics argue that Shakespeare's sisters are too violent and cruel to be believable characters. Joseph Wharton claims, 'Goneril and Regan's savagery is too diabolical to be credible.'

Goneril and Regan present a clear example of their excessive savagery in the blinding of Gloucester in III.7. They come together to work as a vicious team as they participate in the most horrific act in the play. The two sisters appear to be excited: Goneril suggests the method of torture, 'pluck out his eyes!', whereas Regan takes a more controlled approach which may even have a judicial ring to it: 'Hang him instantly!' Any judicious effect is ruined however when the playwright makes her add, 'one side will mock another – th'other too.' This demonstrates how both sisters take pleasure in inflicting pain on Gloucester. To undertake such a gross physical act shows their callous, cruel nature and would leave the audience in shock. The brutality of the blinding is not only a selfish act, but a warning to others. They want others to know that they will do anything to gain power. When Cornwall's servant intervenes to stop the torture of Gloucester, Regan is outraged – 'A peasant stand up thus!' The audience may find this darkly amusing because she has broken her bond of loyalty to her father but gets annoyed when a servant breaks his oath of loyalty to Cornwall and her.

Although the sisters come together to commit malicious felonies like blinding Gloucester, they are both secretly working against each other as they have selfish natures and do not want to share power. When Goneril finds out about the relationship between Regan and Edmund, it is the perfect opportunity for her to get her sister out of the picture. She is driven by the twin motivations of envy of her sister and her lust towards Edmund, to poison her sister, Shakespeare giving the clue in V.3 via the line 'if not, I'll ne'er trust medicine'. Although it appears at first that Goneril has no conscience about killing her sister, she then kills herself. This is not actually a change of character for Goneril as the suicide is not a result of her guilt but an act of resistance to Albany's growing power. Besides, Edmund is dying and so the plan Goneril had of ruling with him has died. Throughout the whole play, corruption, greed and selfishness have been key themes. I think that through the actions of Goneril and Regan, Shakespeare shows his audience how the need for power and the embracing of greed will lead to the breakdown of relationships, both inside and outside the family. The storm could be seen to have been set off by Goneril and Regain in that the kingdom in 'King Lear' is like a small model of the universe. As soon as Lear is betrayed by his daughters, going against the old order of power, nature reacts violently. The storm reflects the turmoil of the kingdom under the power structure of Edmund, Regan and Cornwall before he gets stabbed.

In my opinion, neither daughter has achieved anything like success in their fight for power. The power they have is transitory. The way that Shakespeare shows how the sisters have been socialised makes them competitive and determined but once they have achieved their goals, it leads to their decline, as they seem to go into 'self-destruct' mode. Shakespeare shows the audience that in the end cruelty defeats itself. Shakespeare doesn't explain the sisters' motives at all which is scary.

noisy diversion. Edgar departs and Edmund "cuts his arm" (SD) to "beget opinion" for what he will make appear to be a "more fierce endeavour" (34) than it really was. Some audiences may believe that Edgar runs away on very little prompting, so may be either weak-minded or in thrall to his brother's psychological superiority; however, Lear's abdication has set improbable events in motion and Edgar is perhaps wise to run away from the distressing confusion, not knowing who out of Gloucester, Cornwall or Albany may be truly plotting against him. Edmund's mention of Cornwall's "party 'gainst the Duke of Albany" also points to dangerous factionalism and a potential civil war that Edgar will be wise to avoid until he can discover more.

Gloucester's behaviour in taking Edmund's version of events at face value — "Here he stood in the dark, his sharp sword out, / Mumbling of wicked charms, conjuring the moon" (38–39) — may be similarly unbelievable or even irritating to some audiences: his readiness to believe an illegitimate son hardly known to him can be seen as credulity beyond belief. However, Shakespeare has already taken pains to present Gloucester as superstitious and gullible so it can be argued that his behaviour is in character. His stupidity at believing his disloyal child's lies and his rashness in seeking a stern punishment for his true child mirrors the character and behaviour of Lear in the main plot and so brings a pleasing artistic symmetry to the play. Besides, there was a long-established stage convention that good characters believed wicked ones, partly due to the legacy of medieval morality plays and partly due to a quasi-religious belief that hypocrisy and lying were undetectable.

There is also some darkly delicious comedy in the exchanges between Edmund and Gloucester. Edmund clearly relishes telling the story of Edgar's "unnatural purpose" to his dim father. His account "With his prepared sword, he charges home" sounds as if he were recounting a sporting encounter and his report of his brother's direct speech "Thou unpossessing bastard" is highly unlike any language spoken by Edgar thus far. Yet Gloucester's knowledge of both of his sons' true natures is so imperfect that Edmund's lies prevail and Gloucester effectively disinherits Edgar on line 78 "I never got him", installing Edmund in his place by calling him a "Loyal and natural boy" (a dark irony) and promising he will "work the means / To make thee capable" (lines 84–85). Within the space of only 64 lines between 21 and 85, Edmund has secured Edgar's flight and disinheritance and engineered his own promotion. This has nothing to do with luck: he is already the epitome of the hugely intelligent and dynamic Machiavellian villain.

Examiner's commentary

The candidate's response is confident, insightful and well-illustrated with useful textual references.

- ◥ The essay shows a splendid awareness of the structure of the scene by making excellent use of the chronological sequencing of the plot developments of Act 2 scene 1.

- ◥ The candidate does well to identify that Edmund reacts with intelligence and speed of thought to Curan's revelation that the arrival of Cornwall and Regan is imminent so implies that it is far more than luck that secures Edmund an advantage over his rivals.

- ◥ The point about Edmund's speech to Edgar (lines 21–24) being like a verbal battering is interesting. The impact of the speech – that it leaves Edgar bewildered and all but speechless – is analysed and clearly understood.

- ◥ The candidate makes an excellent point that though some audiences may interpret Edgar as gullible and weak-minded, Lear's sudden and unexpected abdication has set dark and improbable events in motion and due to the rise of factionalism in Britain it may be wise for Edgar to run away so he can discover more about the post-abdication politics before he decides on his best course of action.

- ◥ The candidate demonstrates that she understands that there is more than luck involved in how Edmund tricks both Edgar (who is afraid and nervous) and Gloucester whose superstitious gullibility is already well-known and so can be ruthlessly exploited by his Machiavellian son.

Perhaps the candidate may have created an earlier focus on the notion of luck – as she does with the notion of gullibility – but as the essay is always on task and highly analytical this slight problem with the essay's structure does not detract from its overall merits so the response still deserves a secure A grade reward.

Student E

The second student is responding to the following task:

Russian novelist Leo Tolstoy claimed that when Lear was mad the things he said were "unnatural", "absurd" and were not relevant to the play's major themes. To what extent do you agree with this view in relationship to how madness is presented in Act 3 scene 4?

Remember to include in your answer relevant comment on Shakespeare's dramatic methods.

Tolstoy is clearly correct in his claim that Lear is to some degree unnatural when he is mad: people suffering from the tortures of madness are not renowned for their rational words and calm demeanour: if the old King's behaviour and speech were not unnatural he would not be mad at all. However Tolstoy is in error when he claims that Lear's madness has no relationship to the play's major themes. Lear's madness has been brought about by the monstrous "filial ingratitude" of Goneril and Regan and Shakespeare is very precise in giving the King many wise insights especially about the relationships between society's "haves" and "have nots": he prays not to the gods but to the "Poor naked wretches" (line 28) he ignored when he held power. Both Lear here and later Gloucester in Act 4 scene 1 learn that sharing wealth and privilege more equally will lead to a fairer society. This fair society, however, can only be brought about by the conscious decisions of the wealthy who have a "superflux" or overabundance of riches which they do not need. The privileged elite should have behaved better is the moral. Perhaps such egalitarian thoughts may have sounded absurd and mad in the early seventeenth century but for a modern audience living in the Austerity Britain of 2015 they may appear to be both wise and convincing.

Though his actions and utterings may look and sound mad, Lear's new perspective makes him place the needs of others before his own, thus he makes sure that the Fool enters the hovel before he goes in. Edgar in his disguise as Poor Tom o' Bedlam fascinates Lear whose assumption that only the unkindness of his "pelican daughters" (line 74) could have driven Tom insane surely links to the play's recurrent themes of filial ingratitude and the broken relationships within dysfunctional families. Lear's own pain prompts him to believe that Tom has suffered the same fate as himself: "Didst thou give all to thy two daughters? And art though come to this? (lines 48–49); "...Nothing could have subdued nature / To such a lowness but his unkind daughters" (lines 69–70). Edgar's ranting and gibbering about the "foul fiend", "four inch bridges" and his incessant coldness make the audience feel anxious: we know he is not mad but is just pretending. Pretence and dishonesty are key themes in "King Lear": children pretending to love their parents but who maliciously and cynically abuse and lie to them have been strands in the main plot with Lear, Goneril and Regan and in the sub-plot with Edmund and Gloucester. Tolstoy's analysis seems to miss these key features which are far from irrelevant to the play as a whole.

In both Lear's real and Tom's feigned madness there are strands of reason and logic making some of their comments far from absurd; Lear struggles to make sense of his disintegrating world: "plagues" and animal savagery (his daughters are "pelicans") torment his brain but in spite of what Tolstoy says Lear's stream of consciousness follows a sort of logic: "flesh" begets children who will be cruel (lines 73–74). When Lear announces that "Unaccommodated man is no more but such a poor, bare, forked animal as thou art" (lines 105–06) and the stage directions reveal that he tears at his own clothes, the audience sees what it is to be human when all the trappings of wealth and status have been stripped away. When we are driven to distraction human beings are vulnerable, lonely, frightened and tormented by memories of cruelties we have inflicted on others and which have been inflicted on us. Tough Tolstoy is correct that Lear's behaviour is "'unnatural" because it is unusual; Shakespeare makes it clear that the impact of his madness on the audience is far from absurd because it is always relevant to the play's major themes.

Examiner's commentary

This candidate has the confidence to disagree with a famous figure in world literature and present her own analyses in a comprehensive and clear answer which shows very good understanding of how madness is presented in Act 3 scene 4.

◤ The answer acknowledges that Tolstoy may be correct in one observation (Lear's speech is unnatural in the sense that it is unusual) but that his other claims about Lear's speech being absurd and irrelevant to some of the play's major themes are unfounded. Thus the candidate shows that she has thought very carefully about the totality of Tolstoy's claims and has only rejected two of the three claims put forward.

◤ The essay shows a refreshing sense of the play being open to different interpretations over time: Lear's growing sense of egalitarianism may have been considered mad or absurd in Shakespeare's lifetime but may appear to be wise and true today. This awareness of historicism adds to the essay's many qualities.

> ◥ The essay is aware of the play as a dramatic construct and references to what the audience sees on stage and to various stage directions show that the candidate has a very clear understanding of genre.

The essay is perhaps a little short for an A-level response but the clarity of ideas, the knowledge and understanding shown, the use of textual detail and the sense of the candidate's own informed, personal voice being communicated to the reader are all evidence that this work has all of the hallmarks of grade A.

Extended commentary

What does the final act of *King Lear* add to the audience's understanding of Shakespeare's presentation of the nature of Edmund?

It is possible to analyse Edmund as a character dealt a bad hand by Fate, forced by the circumstances of his illegitimacy to inhabit the hinterlands of aristocratic life, living on whatever scraps his father Gloucester chooses to throw his way while his 'legitimate' brother Edgar is free to enjoy the high social status of the first-born male heir and all of the attendant privileges of inherited wealth. Yet such an interpretation would disgust Edmund, who is presented by Shakespeare from the beginning as the rebellious outsider who scornfully rejects the views expounded by his superstitious father that God (or the gods) makes the stars move in their preordained manner and thus is responsible for the fortunes of mankind. Such a view is cowardly in Edmund's eyes because it offers an excuse for bad behaviour. Today people who do not wish to take full responsibility for their own actions can blame 'society' or their upbringing; in a similar way in Jacobean England people could blame their vices on the influence of the stars rather than accepting that crimes, sins and misdemeanours were the consequences of their own willed actions. Edmund explains it thus:

'...when we are sick in fortune, often the surfeits of our own behaviour, we make guilty of our disasters the sun, the moon and the stars, as if we were villains on necessity ... drunkards, liars and adulterers by an enforced obedience of planetary influence ... Fut! I should have been that I am had the maidenliest star in the firmament twinkled on my bastardizing.' (1.2.119–33)

So from his second dazzling soliloquy in 1:2 Edmund offers the audience a further insight into his nature: he chooses wickedness; he has not had it thrust upon him. A true Machiavellian, his behaviour is expedient and undertaken for political and personal gain. His actions are his own, distilled in the cauldron of his own resentful and ambitious heart: 'Let me, if not by birth, have lands by wit; / All with me's meet that I can fashion fit' (lines 181–82). Edmund is determined to rise in the world: and will stop at nothing to achieve his ambition. Audiences can like Edmund because he stands out in the open as the architect of his own fate, never hiding behind weak superstition to excuse his behaviour. So is it a surprise that in the play's final scene Edmund relents and attempts to save Lear's and Cordelia's lives after having been the one to give the orders for their deaths?

At the beginning of 5:3 Edmund is clearly the man in charge, instructing the captain to follow the murderous orders in his written note. He even offers some philosophical advice: 'men / Are as the time is: to be tender-minded / Does not become the sword.' This little speech is revealing in two ways. The first way is that the note proves Edmund's continued reliance on the written word: he has duped his father and furthered his seduction of Goneril and Regan via carefully constructed, persuasive letters. The speech is also important in the way it further demonstrates Edmund's intellectual nature: he inverts the usual phrase 'tender-hearted' into 'tender-minded' thus revealing that Edmund's actions are motivated more by what he thinks than what he feels. Therefore the rest of Edmund's behaviour in Act V scene 3 is not surprising as his 'wickedness' has only ever been the result of an intellectual commitment to self-interest, in contrast to Goneril's and Regan's non-intellectual, more primitive, less rational wickedness. When the scene plays out and Edmund realises that in Machiavellian terms he can progress no further, he has no intellectual reason to be cruel and therefore stops.

The action on stage after Lear's and Cordelia's exit crackles with tension, largely centred around Edmund's sexual charisma: Albany's entrance reminds the audience of Goneril's compromising letter to Edmund, tucked away in Albany's doublet and bound to be produced at some point. Regan's confession (lines 76–79) that she and all her possessions now belong to her new 'lord and master' Edmund brings the ménage-a-trois to its climax. The sight of the sisters brazenly squabbling in front of Albany over who will 'enjoy' Edmund is great theatre, as is the discovery that Goneril has poisoned Regan who will not live to marry her new master. Albany's dark sense of humour creates gritty comic relief as he tells the 'half-blooded fellow': 'If you will marry, make your love to me; / My lady is bespoke' (lines 89–90).

Yet throughout the scene the playwright is careful to create an aura of nobility about Edmund despite his many vices: before attempting to arrest him for treason, Albany praises Edmund's 'valiant strain' in battle. Edmund's acceptance of trial by combat can be interpreted as a noble gesture: chivalric codes do not require a gentleman to defend his honour against an anonymous, masked accuser. Edmund's personal bravery as a warrior is never in doubt. His willingness to fight may be viewed as 'uncharacteristic sentimentalism' (Robert Heilman, 'This Great Stage: Image and Structure in "King Lear"') but it is more probably down to Edmund's boundless confidence. Following the duel the brothers exchange forgiveness and the playwright is very careful to make the defeated Edmund the first to offer forgiveness, with the lines 'If thou'rt noble, I do forgive thee'. Edmund responds to Edgar's account of his vicissitudes in the acknowledgement 'This speech of yours hath moved me, / And shall perchance do good' (lines 198–99), and so the audience perceives a change in Edmund's behaviour though not, perhaps, his philosophy. His imminent death means he can gain no further political advantage in the 'gored state' and his intellect tells him the deaths of Lear and Cordelia are now unnecessary for his own advancement. He is still a villain to an extent, taking pride in his power over women: when Goneril's and Regan's bodies are brought on stage he has time to say 'Yet Edmund was beloved' before he arranges for Lear and Cordelia to be saved in line 243. He still understands his 'own nature' to be as it always was – 'rough', 'lecherous' as he acknowledged in Act I, and ambitious throughout – but wants to do some good despite that nature. His final words are not a plea for understanding or forgiveness but a stark confession of his crimes against Cordelia. He sent the captain 'To hang Cordelia in the prison and / To lay the blame upon her own despair, / That she fordid herself' (251–53). The dying Edmund does not squeal, beg or pray to gods he does not believe in. In his death he is defeated but unbowed; he dies as he lived: a calculated rationalist committed to the tenets of Free Will.

Before studying this section, you should identify your own 'top ten quotations' – i.e. those lines that seem to capture a key theme or aspect of the text most aptly and memorably – and clearly identify what it is about your choices that makes each one so significant. No two readers of *King Lear* will select exactly the same set and it will be well worth discussing (and perhaps even having to defend) your choices with other students. When you have done this, look carefully at the following list of 'Top ten quotations' (some of which are shortened versions of longer speeches) and consider each one's possible significance within the play. How might each be used in an essay response to support your exploration of various elements or readings of *King Lear*? Consider what these quotations tell us about Shakespeare's ideas, themes and methods, as well as how far they may contribute to various potential ways of interpreting the text.

1

LEAR: …what can you say to draw
                        A third more opulent than your sisters'? Speak!
CORDELIA: …Nothing, my lord.
LEAR: Nothing?
CORDELIA: Nothing.
LEAR: How, nothing will come of nothing. Speak again.
(I.1.85–90)

◀ Lear expects Cordelia to be able to outdo Goneril's and Regan's flattery in the love-test but is given an answer he neither wants nor expects to hear, encapsulated in the vitally important word 'Nothing', repeated by father and daughter five times in four lines, like an echo. In contrast to the hollow sycophancy of Goneril and Regan, Cordelia goes on to give her father a truthful evaluation of her love: she loves him according to her 'bond'; that is, she understands and accepts her duty to love him as a father and king but cannot lie by pretending the relationship goes beyond what is appropriate and natural.

EDMUND: Thou, Nature, art my goddess; to thy law
         My services are bound.
               …Why bastard? Wherefore base?
         When my dimensions are as well compact,
         My mind as generous and my shape as true
         As honest madam's issue? Why brand they us
         With 'base'? with 'baseness', 'bastardy'? 'Base, base'?
               …Well, then,
         Legitimate Edgar, I must have your land.
                …I grow, I prosper:
         Now gods, stand up for bastards!

(I.2.1–22)

▼ This is an extract from the first soliloquy in the play and is important in terms of characterisation and theme. Edmund, fairly bouncing on to the stage with swaggering confidence, sets about raising himself by the force of his own independent free will. As with the repetition of the word 'Nothing' in Act I scene 1, Shakespeare repeats several words that link to the play's themes of legitimacy versus bastardy: the repetition of the key noun 'bastard' and the two adjectives 'base' and 'legitimate' reveal Edmund's obsession with his own 'whoreson' status in contrast to his brother's enviable status as Gloucester's rightful heir. This soliloquy demonstrates Edmund's resentment at and disgust with the social order. Shakespeare makes him invoke 'Nature', personified as his goddess, to show the audience how anarchic and truly terrifying he can be: he is the epitome of the malcontent pagan renouncing Christianity and conformity. To some, he is 'Hamlet with testosterone'.

Context

It is interesting to note that the word 'dimensions' is used in the same context in *The Atheist's Tragedy* – 'Me thinks, my parts, and my dimensions are/As many, as large, as well compos'd as his' (spoken by D'Amville in Act V scene 2). This play, about which scholars contest the authorship (some claim Cyril Tourneur, others Thomas Middleton), came after *King Lear*.

D'Amville, the eponymous atheist, shares a similar view of Nature with Edmund in *King Lear*: both men deny that there is a power stronger than visible nature and deliberately live outside conventional Christian moral codes. Edmund, once the game is up, tries to save Cordelia; D'Amville 'strikes out his own brains' on the scaffold after learning that there is a 'power' above Nature.

3

LEAR:
                              I am a man
More sinned against than sinning.
(III.2.59–60)

> Lear, battered by the storm and on the verge of nervous collapse due to the misdemeanours of Goneril and Regan, shows that he is slowly coming to terms with the idea of appropriate balance. He acknowledges his grave error in banishing Cordelia as early as I.5.24 when he says 'I did her wrong', but feels that his punishment at being cast out is inappropriately harsh. Shakespeare couches this acknowledgement in the language of Christianity, showing that despite the apparently pagan environment of the play, Lear inhabits an inner world of sin, guilt and retribution. He is still full of anger. He still rails. He gives in to self-pity. He is, however, slowly developing the perspective to allow him to make better judgements and 'see better'.

4

LEAR:
Poor naked wretches, wheresoe'er you are,
That bide the pelting of this pitiless storm,
How shall your houseless heads and unfed sides,
Your looped and windowed raggedness, defend you
From seasons such as these? O, I have ta'en
Too little care of this. Take physic, pomp…
(III.4.28–33)

> Though Tolstoy cited this speech as evidence of Lear giving vent to 'incessant pompous raving', it is a vital moment in the play, in which Lear shows that his own sufferings have taught him to consider society's outcasts and that when he enjoyed the pomp of kingship he ignored such poor wretches. It is simultaneously a confession of Lear's own previous selfishness and a criticism of Shakespeare's society. This is a powerful speech of repentance, a necessary stage on the path to redemption, and demonstrates the ongoing development of Lear's morality from quotation 3.

5

LEAR:
Is man no more than this? Consider him well. Thou ow'st the worm no silk, the beast no hide, the sheep no wool, the cat no perfume. Ha? Here's three on's us are sophisticated; thou art the thing itself. Unaccommodated man is no more but such a poor, bare, forked animal as thou art.
(III.4.101–06)

> This is one of the sections of *King Lear* most closely linked to Montaigne, with Shakespeare amalgamating several passages found in Florio. Lear has lost everything, but in the process has gained a profound insight: that man without his trappings of power and wealth is a poor, naked animal. This is a shocking and disturbing thought for traditionalists who hold to the notions of order and degree. If man is an animal, he has no soul to save. This was an anarchic thought for the early seventeenth century.

GLOUCESTER: As flies to wanton boys are we to the gods,
They kill us for their sport.
(IV.1.38–39)

6

> Montaigne, quoting Plautus, said much the same thing: 'The gods do reckon and racket us men as their tennis balls.' Students need to decide whether this is Shakespeare's own view, as many critics aver, or whether it represents the subjective view of the suicidal Gloucester at this stage of the play. Certainly Gloucester suffers in profound despair at this juncture and believes that there is no justice in the universe, that we are powerless in our quest to find rationality and justice in life and that there is only the 'sport' of inscrutable gods, who exist beyond our human abilities of comprehension, seeming to reward cruelty and to delight in making us suffer. Careful students will note the irony of this second reference of Gloucester's to 'sport': the first was when he was recounting his youthful sexual exploits to Kent. Sport had an appeal when Gloucester enjoyed adultery; now, as a pawn in the gods' game, he is driven to distraction.

KENT: It is the stars,
The stars above us govern our conditions,
Else one self mate and make could not beget
Such different issues.
(IV.3.33–35)

7

> Kent, overwhelmed by Cordelia's forgiving and saintly nature, philosophises on the nature of the human character. Goneril and Regan share the same biological father as Cordelia, so Kent is forced to conclude that our natures as well as our fortunes lie in the stars, controlled by God through the machinations of the Great Chain of Being. This is the orthodox view of the influence of the stars (Gloucester believes it until his faith in the good gods is shattered) and it is gleefully satirised by Edmund in I.2.118–33.

LEAR: …a dog's obeyed in office …
Through tattered clothes great vices do appear;
Robes and furred gowns hide all.
(IV.6.154–61)

8

> Lear in his madness reveals some of his most profound insights. Once again Shakespeare has a debt to Montaigne, who wrote in the *Essays*: 'There are Nations who receive and admit a Dogge to be their King.' The theme of the outward show of authority hiding a multitude of sins is echoed by Shakespeare in *Measure for Measure*, when Angelo says:

O place, O form,

How often dost thou with thy case, thy habit,

Wrench awe from fools and tie the wiser souls

To thy false seeming!

(II.4.12–15)

▾ The moral of both quotations is that we are fools if we are swayed by what we find on the outside of things: *all that glisters is not gold*. Authority is an illusion: our superiors are corrupt but cover it up in the trappings of wealth. Shakespeare was expressing dangerous political sentiments for his time.

9

LEAR: Thou must be patient. We came crying hither:
Thou knowst the first time that we smell the air
We wawl and cry.
(IV.6.174–76)

▾ Lear, just moments after recognising Gloucester, has more wisdom to impart. The old king, still mad, has finally learned patience in the face of a human condition that is absurd. Life is a struggle and we will be miserable all the while we are alive, from the very first moment of our existence.

10

LEAR: You do me wrong to take me out o'the grave.
Thou art a soul in bliss, but I am bound
Upon a wheel of fire that mine own tears
Do scald like molten lead …
I fear I am not in my perfect mind.
Methinks I should know you …
For, as I am a man, I think this lady
To be my child Cordelia.
CORDELIA: And so I am, I am.
(IV.7.45–70)

▾ The relationship between Lear and Cordelia has come full circle. Gone are the bombastic threats and unnatural curses of Act I scene 1. The language is also significantly different to that used by the playwright in Lear's raving scenes: here the language is almost entirely monosyllabic. The diction is simple and lucid and most tender when Lear's daughter is recognised no longer as 'this lady' but as 'my child Cordelia'. Lear's previous notion was that she was a spirit, 'a soul in bliss', while he was 'bound upon a wheel of fire' – reminiscent of medieval images of hell as well as Fortune's Wheel. Now, however, he and Cordelia do not occupy the different extremities of creation (heaven and hell) but are together, reconciled in a moment of human domesticity that features music, rest and tenderness. Lear can be seen to represent a kind of prodigal father coming home to his loving daughter. Yet the happiness is all too brief. Act V, with its tragic horrors, awaits.

Books

▼ Ackroyd, P. (2005) *Shakespeare: The Biography*, Chatto & Windus.

- Hugely entertaining and full of Ackroyd's unique analyses, this account of Shakespeare's life is intuitive and imaginative.

▼ Bloom, H. (1999) *Shakespeare: The Invention of the Human*, Fourth Estate.

- Bloom savages what he calls 'The School of Resentment': feminists, new historicists and cultural materialists who have 'appropriated' Shakespeare Studies in recent years. Firmly focussed on considerations of character, Bloom claims that Shakespeare 'invented' human personality as we know it: intriguing, bombastic, refreshingly cavalier.

▼ Greenblatt, S. (2004) *Will in the World: How Shakespeare Became Shakespeare*, Jonathan Cape.

- In some ways as speculative as Ackroyd's biography, Greenblatt the new historicist brilliantly takes us through Shakespeare's life and career.

▼ Gurr, A. (1992) *The Shakespearean Stage 1574–1642*, CUP.

- Lively, informative and reliable, Gurr's book is the best guide to the theatre of Shakespeare's time, containing detailed descriptions of the acting companies, their practices, the staging and the audiences.

▼ Hotson, L. (1952) *Shakespeare's Motley*, OUP.

- An entertaining if slightly dated account of Shakespeare's fools.

▼ Kermode, F. (1969) *Shakespeare – King Lear: A Casebook*, Macmillan.

- A very interesting collection of critical essays.

▼ Kermode, F. (2001) *Shakespeare's Language*, Penguin.

- Kermode argues that between 1594 and 1608 Shakespeare became a different kind of poet whose language was – even in his own time – difficult and muscular, a 'representation of excited, anxious thought.

▼ Nicholl, C. (2008) *The Lodger: Shakespeare on Silver Street*, Penguin.

- This is a brilliant example of micro-research: around 1604 Shakespeare lodged in Silver Street with the Mountjoys, a French Huguenot family and the playwright became involved in the betrothal of Mary Mountjoy, the daughter, to Stephen Belott, Mr Mountjoy's apprentice – perhaps acting as a witness. In 1612 Mountjoy was accused of reneging on the dowry, and Shakespeare had to give evidence. Genuinely fascinating.

▼ Pritchard, K. (2011) 'Legitimacy, Illegitimacy and Sovereignty in Shakespeare's British Plays', University of Manchester PhD thesis.

- A readable and informative analysis of illegitimacy that makes some pertinent observations about Edmund, as well as wider society.

- Ralli, A. (1974) *A History of Shakespearean Criticism Vols 1 & 2*, Humanities Press.

  – This is an overview of the major criticism of Shakespeare's plays between his own lifetime and 1925; great as a companion to the Casebook.

- Reese, M.M. (1964) *Shakespeare, His World and His Work*, Edward Arnold.

  – First printed in 1953 and notably reprinted in 1964, this is one of the better-written and researched biographies before Schoenbaum's classic.

- Salingar, L. (1974) *Shakespeare and the Traditions of Comedy*, CUP.

  – Salingar traces the links between Shakespeare's comedies and earlier Greek and Roman traditions: useful background for an analysis of the Fool.

- Schoenbaum, S. (1975) *William Shakespeare: A Documentary Life*, OUP.

  – A fact and document-filled tour-de-force that remains the essential starting-point for those interested in Shakespeare biography.

- Thomson, P. (1992) *Shakespeare's Professional Career*, CUP.

  – Thomson explains Shakespeare's writing career year by year.

- Wells, S. (1994) *Shakespeare: A Dramatic Life*, Sinclair-Stevenson.

  – A review of all the plays and poems, Wells places Shakespeare's writing against what we know of his life. There is much of interest about productions of the plays with frequent references to modern theatre.

Websites and films

http://shakespeare.mit.edu –Shakespeare's Complete Works.

www.bl.uk/treasures/shakespeare/homepage.html –This is the British Library website and is a national treasure. Cherish it.

http://internetshakespeare.uvic.ca/Library/plays/Lr.html –This website allows users to examine in detail the text of *King Lear* Q1.

www.shakespeare-online.com –This is a very user-friendly and comprehensive resource with hundreds of links.

1983: ITV production of *King Lear*, directed by Michael Elliott, with a fine performance by Laurence Olivier, frail but resilient after serious illness (158m).

1971: Columbia Pictures version, directed by Peter Brook and starring Paul Scofield. It is a reprise of the much-lauded RSC production of 1962 and is bold and highly stylised. The film was cut to 132 minutes to highlight the dark and cruel aspects of the play, and was shot in black and white.

1982: Jonathan Miller directed the play for the BBC and chose a dark, austere set. This version of the play, is the closest to Shakespeare's original script (183m).